MODERN MUZZLELOADING
FOR TODAY'S
WHITETAILS

BY
IAN MCMURCHY

EDITOR
PATRICK DURKIN

MANAGING EDITOR
DAVE BEAUCHAINE

PHOTOGRAPHY BY
IAN MCMURCHY
UNLESS NOTED OTHERWISE

Book design by Allen West, Krause Publications.

Cover Credits:
Photos by Ian McMurchy

Published by

 **krause publications**
The World's Largest Hobby and Collectibles Publisher

700 E. State St. • Iola, WI 54990-0001

Please call or write for our free catalog of publications. Our toll-free number to
place an order or to obtain a free catalog is (800) 258-0929. Please use our regular
business telephone (715) 445-2214 for editorial comment and further information.
Library of Congress Catalog Number: 00-102-689
ISBN: 0-87341-951-0
Printed in the United States of America

This book is dedicated to the women in my life:

my wife, Darlene;

my mother, Marjorie;

my beautiful daughters, Heather, Katherine and Joanna;

and my future daughter, Chantelle.

I am a thorn among roses.

Contents

The author's son and hunting buddy, Glen, shares the excitement of a big whitetail with his fiancee Chantelle. Glen and Ian McMurchy spend a lot of time shooting, testing and hunting with in-line muzzleloaders.

Acknowledgments

I am blessed to have a shooting partner who puts up with my cranky days and my fussy ways. This best buddy is also my only son, Glen. My proudest hunting moments are shared with him, despite the fact he manages to shoot bigger and better animals than I do. Thanks, Buddy.

Glen and I are fortunate to have a hunting buddy who makes each hunt an experience and a lot of fun. That man is "Chopper," also known as Richard Hutchinson. Chopper is a special friend, and he, Glen and Jack Keel are charter members of our "Mid-Morning Outfitters" group.

I must also acknowledge some terrific manufacturers and company officials who enable me to test and hunt with their in-line rifles. I was fortunate to meet Tony Knight a long time ago, and he and Bruce Watley arranged for me to shoot every Knight Rifle model that Modern Muzzleloading Inc. has introduced. Similarly, Gregg Ritz and Sherry Fears at Thompson/Center Arms have provided fantastic support and given me access to T/C's prototypes and newest in-lines. Gregg is a dynamo to keep up with, but I try my best. Thanks also to the Frenches — Ken and Ernie — for sharing their knowledge. I also thank the Hodgdon Co., and Chris Hodgdon, in particular, for providing much of the powder I turned into white smoke while researching this book.

I also thank everyone in the muzzleloading industry for their kind assistance and never-ending advice. I work with many companies, and I can truly say everyone has treated me fairly, professionally and with the kind of respect that fosters friendship.

Lastly, I acknowledge a good friend who hopefully made this book more readable and enjoyable: Patrick Durkin, editor of *Deer & Deer Hunting* magazine. Pat loves hunting and sharing the hunt's rewards with his children as much as I do. It doesn't get any better.

Why Hunt Whitetails with an In-Line?

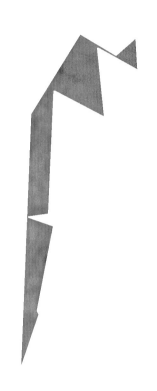

Since its reinvention in the mid-1980s, the in-line muzzleloader has been blessed with good fortune. At the same time of their massive acceptance by deer hunters, these new muzzleloading rifles were complemented perfectly by a variety of saboted bullets and Pyrodex powders.

ead down, my friend Chopper carefully placed each paw as he inched forward on hands and knees. Cautiously moving his legs, Chopper slowly put his weight down to minimize the chance of any sound. The big hunter cradled his imaginary muzzleloader in the bend of his arm, ensuring the muzzle was not pointed toward the ground. Looking forward, he spotted the buck coming toward him on the same trail on which he was crawling! With great care, Chopper sat back on his haunches and slowly shouldered his rifle.

The silence in our office — Chopper's theater — was complete. Secretaries and clerks watched in dumb-struck awe as their magnum-sized boss played out his recent adventure. When he replayed and made his shot on the buck, everyone was happy. Then they thanked him and congratulated him on the great story he had just shared. Finally, they resumed their coffee-break. My buddy got up from the carpeted floor, still basking in the excitement of his first muzzleloading deer kill.

The Excitement of Muzzleloading

I often wonder how many deer hunts are re-enacted in office break rooms across North America each autumn. The excitement Chopper relayed in this true story shows just how much fun black-powder hunting can be. He had never shot a muzzleloader in his life before making that memorable hunt. After I had suggested we hunt the muzzleloader season and offered to supply the equipment, Chopper agreed to give it a try. We practiced the day before opening morning, with me teaching him how to load and fire the shiny new Knight MK-85. As the hunt

Today's average in-line shooter is primarily interested in gaining more deer hunting opportunities and is far less interested in muzzleloading's history and rich, historical traditions. As a result, sales of sidehammer rifles, right, have slumped and now make up a fraction of their former sales.

unfolded the next day, Chopper met with a few frustrations — also known as buck-fever — when he was readying for his first shot at a live whitetail. He quickly overcame the embarrassment of missing a 20-yard standing broadside shot and went on to take that well-earned buck. Since that day, Chopper has become an excellent muzzleloading hunter. He has harvested many deer for his freezer, including a trophy buck or two.

Black-powder hunting with in-line muzzleloaders started in the mid-1980s, and literally exploded onto the hunting scene in the 1990s. Millions of deer hunters fell in love with the in-lines, and manufacturers rushed to meet the surging demand. Wildlife agencies responded by introducing or expanding muzzleloading seasons, which further increased public interest. Black-powder shooting and hunting changed and evolved in ways that earlier participants could never have anticipated. Some of these changes worried and angered many traditionalists, who could only watch as the "primitive" nature of muzzleloading virtually vanished in a handful of years.

As the use of modern muzzleloaders snowballed, the number of traditional black-powder participants dwindled. Flintlocks and sidehammer percussion rifles had long appealed to hunters who enjoyed investing much time, effort and historical apprecia-

tion into their traditional muzzleloaders. For many of these hunters, just shooting their rifles was nearly as important as hunting with these smokepoles. These folks enjoyed improvising tools, accessories and components. They frequently built their rifles from kits that required much handwork. Leather outfits and accouterments of bygone days were common at black-powder shooting events.

In-Lines Dominate the Market

Those days remain popular with many people, but they're slowly fading away. The in-line muzzleloader now rules supreme, especially among those whose primary motivation is deer hunting, not muzzleloading. I expect a future generation someday might only relate the in-line to "muzzleloader shooting." Although this rapid transformation to an in-line world is a fact of life, muzzleloading still provides a great challenge to participants, whether they're modern or traditional shooters.

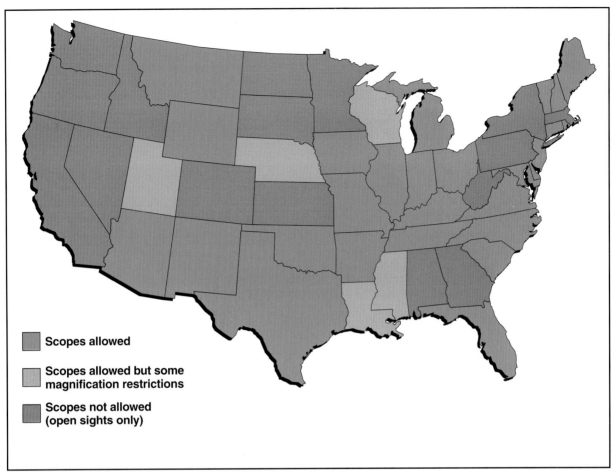

Scopes allowed

Scopes allowed but some magnification restrictions

Scopes not allowed (open sights only)

Figure 1-1. Riflescopes are the preferred sight of the throngs of baby-boomer hunters, who very likely grew up shooting mainly with scopes. Unfortunately, optics are also the battle line drawn between traditional and modern muzzleloaders, and some states don't allow scopes for their black-powder seasons. Others allow only 1X or red-dot scopes during black-powder seasons.

As in-line muzzleloaders became increasingly popular with hunters, sales of sidehammer rifles slumped and now make up a fraction of their former sales. Thompson/Center Arms, manufacturer of some of the finest traditional styled replica muzzleloaders, began offering in-line designs in 1992. By 1995, its sales of in-line rifles exceeded the sales of sidehammer rifles for the first time in T/C's history. Today, traditional muzzleloaders account for less than 20 percent of new sales for T/C, and this number is declining every year.

What is responsible for the in-line popularity surge? Today's average in-line shooter is primarily interested in gaining more hunting opportunities and is less interested in muzzleloading's history and traditions. In fact, many muzzleloading participants are just as interested in hunting deer with bows, shotguns and centerfire rifles. Even so, after they get a taste of shooting in-line muzzleloaders, many of them switch solely to muzzleloading.

Although in-line pistols and shotguns have appeared in the marketplace, they've never achieved the popularity of rifles. Why? Generally, they're not designed for deer hunting, and deer hunting is the No. 1 force in the hunting market. Most people who

buy in-line rifles don't much care about the technicalities of faster, more direct ignition systems or stronger action designs. Most shooters appreciate the fact that in-lines are more user-friendly and more closely resemble the modern firearms they use for deer hunting. They're smitten by the scopes, camo composite stocks, stainless steel barrels and easy-loading sabots that are a big part of the in-line allure. This makes the rifles a convenient match for additional deer hunting during black-powder seasons.

Centerfire rifle converts find that in-lines handle much like the lever- or bolt-actions they've long carried. Besides, they never considered birds-eye maple stocks, long barrels, inletted patch boxes and curved metal butt plates essential on black-powder hunting rifles.

The ease of mounting riflescopes is one of the

Hunters choosing an in-line must decide on caliber. The .50-caliber rifle, which the author's son, Glen, used to take this buck, is the most popular. Sales of this caliber are 10 times that of the .54 bore. The author thinks the .50-caliber rifle is best for whitetails, and makes an excellent all-around caliber.

preferred sight of the throngs of baby-boomer hunters, who very likely grew up shooting mainly with scopes. For them, in-lines and scopes go hand-in-glove. In addition, these middle-aged hunters have the time and money to get into a new type of hunting. And besides, by the time they took up in-lines, many of these people are or were at an age where optics became a necessity.

Unfortunately, optics are also the battle line drawn between traditional and modern muzzleloaders, and some states don't allow scopes for their black-powder seasons (see Figure 1-1). Some states have relaxed that restriction a bit by allowing 1X or red-dot scopes, which have no magnification. The 1X scopes are easier to use than iron sights, especially for those whose eyesight isn't what it used to be.

Choosing a Caliber

When choosing an in-line rifle, should you buy a .50- or .54-caliber gun? This is probably the first decision you must make when buying an in-line. With the advent of saboted bullets, .50-caliber rifles are by far the most popular. In fact, .50-caliber sales run at about a 10-1 ratio or more over the bigger .54 bore. Many experienced shooters find that the .50-caliber loads shoot slightly more accurately on paper, particularly with the popular sabot/bullet loads. This is probably because the .50-caliber sabots have thinner petals or side panels, and therefore release their encased bullets more uniformly. Hunters interested solely in hunting North America's largest deer — namely, elk and moose — might prefer the .54 bore because it can shoot the heavier conical bullets and slightly heavier sabot/bullet combinations. However, I consider that the only advantage of the .54 bore, because most saboted loads use identical bullets and bullet weights in both calibers. Many in-line shooters use saboted bullets up to 300 or 325 grains in either caliber for big-game hunting.

biggest advantages of in-lines over traditional rifles. Scopes ensure more accurate shooting, regardless of the firearm on which they're mounted. Scopes are preferred by serious hunters and, because many people who buy in-lines are hunters first and black-powder enthusiasts second, they aren't concerned about breaking with tradition. Scopes are the

Advanced Systems

Since its reinvention in the mid-1980s, the in-line muzzleloader has been blessed with good fortune. At the same time of their massive acceptance by deer hunters, other developments surfaced to complement and enhance the new rifles. Among these advancements are saboted bullets, Pyrodex pellets, better ignition systems, modern cleaning solvents and laser-equipped rangefinders. All these items played major roles in advancing the in-line revolution. These products are superb hunting tools that are well-suited for hunting white-tailed deer. Muzzleloading deer hunters have never had it so good.

As with the in-line itself, the idea of saboted bullets goes back a long time. But with the advent of modern plastics and manufacturing methods, the sabot has been perfected in recent years. Saboted bullets are the preferred projectile of most in-line hunters because of their vastly improved performance over conical bullets. Throw in an improved, more consistent propellant, and it's clear why in-lines so easily captured the muzzleloading market.

Black powder, of course, is the oldest propellant

Other muzzleloading developments played a major role in advancing the in-line revolution. Among these advancements are saboted bullets, better ignition systems, modern cleaning solvents, and consistent, easy-to-use propellants.

known to man. Black powder works well for its intended purpose, and it served mankind well for centuries. Unfortunately, black powder is an explosive and can be extremely dangerous. Modern smokeless gunpowder, however, is classified as a combustible product. Smokeless powder does not detonate or explode unless confined, whereas black powder goes off with a bang whenever it's ignited.

In addition, black-powder residue has the annoying property of attracting moisture and causing rust. Smokeless residue is relatively inert. The difference is significant. Smokeless powder has far fewer restrictions and regulations covering its storage and use, and it's more "user-friendly." Therefore, manufacturers such as the Hodgdon Powder Co. have developed black-powder substitutes that blended desirable properties of each powder. Hodgdon's Pyrodex

Although loading a muzzleloader is a simple procedure, differences in swabbing frequency, powder amount, sabot type and seating pressure can affect shot-to-shot accuracy. The key to muzzleloading accuracy is consistency of your techniques and the components.

powder retains the low-energy yield and billowing white smoke of black powder. Pyrodex is classified as a combustible, and it has less tendency to cause rust. This gives in-line hunters the best of both worlds, which is why most of them prefer Pyrodex and other black-powder substitutes.

An interesting situation unfolded as the in-line rifle boomed in popularity with North America's deer hunters. The Hodgdon Powder Co. introduced 50-grain compressed pellets, which are made from its Pyrodex powder. The timing of the pellet's introduction could not have been better planned. Call it luck or good fortune, the pellets were an immediate hit with hunters, and created so much demand that Hodgdon initially suffered huge production headaches. Within a year of the pellet's introduction, however, Hodgdon was able to meet demands and bring out other options, such as the 30-grain pellet.

Ignitions and Cleaning Systems

Manufacturers constantly look to improve their products. But because in-lines are such simple firearms, engineers have few options to play with and modify. One element that offered potentials for improved performance, however, was the ignition system. Manufacturers were soon tinkering with the standard nipple and breech-plug designs while examining several ignition devices to improve accuracy, consistency and reliability. Hunters can now choose between No. 11 percussion caps, musket caps and the modern 209 shotgun primers for touching off their charges. And more advances are on the horizon, such as the electronic ignitions, first introduced in commercial centerfire rifles in January 2000.

Another major technological advancement was the creation of many new chemicals to simplify maintenance and gun-cleaning tasks. The hassle of cleaning black-powder hunting rifles was one reason many hunters avoided them for deer hunting. Boiling water, grimy metal and noxious fumes were a big part of muzzleloading's "charm." And rust was a constant, never-say-quit enemy. Enter modern science. Cleaning and protecting black-powder guns became nearly as simple as maintaining any other

type of firearm. The biggest difference between maintaining a centerfire rifle and a muzzleloading rifle is that smokepoles must be cleaned immediately after their use. Constantly improving propellants might eventually eliminate the rust problem, but until then, shooters must ensure that corrosive residue is removed promptly.

How Good are They?

Just how good are the new in-line muzzleloaders? Most manufacturers promise hunters centerfire-rifle accuracy from their in-lines. Many advertisements show three-shot groups of 2 inches or less at 100 yards. Higher velocities and resultant higher energy yields generated further comparisons to centerfire rifles, with some companies touting "7 mm Magnum energies!" That kind of performance, plus the promise of minimum-maintenance requirements, inspired countless hunters to buy in-lines.

Unfortunately, rumors and misinformation resulted from the notion that in-lines are "super guns." These misconceptions hampered the in-line movement, but more on that later.

Are 2-inch groups the accuracy norm, and is such shooting attainable by just about any deer hunter?

Many muzzleloading rifles only perform to their full potential when using a specific load and loading procedure. That's why in-line shooters must spend a lot of time at the range fine-tuning their hunting loads.

With any muzzleloader, accuracy depends on many more variables than with cartridge-based firearms. Because each shot with a muzzleloader is "the ultimate handload," consistency in techniques and components is extremely important. Loading an in-line is relatively simple, but variables such as swabbing frequency, powder amount, sabot type, seating pressure, swabbing-patch moisture and conical bullet lube can greatly affect an in-line's accuracy. Developing a consistent load and loading procedure is vital. Developing and maintaining the skill and ability to shoot well are also part of the game. In-line shooters must remember what improves and what hurts accuracy. Unlike centerfire firearms, which shoot reasonably well with out-of-the-box factory ammunition, many in-line muzzleloaders only perform to their full potential when using specific loads and loading procedures. That's why it's critical for in-line shooters to spend a lot of time at the rifle range fine-tuning their hunting loads.

Most muzzleloading rifles offer better hunting accuracy than the average slug-shooting smoothbore shotgun, but it's up to the owner to take the time to discover an in-line's full potential.

Enhancing a Hunt's Opportunities

Many special muzzleloading seasons take place in early fall when the weather is mild and deer are in pre-rut patterns, which include regular feeding sessions. Even with the amazing in-line surge in popularity, hunter numbers remain modest when compared to participants in regular firearms and, in some cases, archery, seasons. Opportunities are nearly boundless for hunters who do their homework. In addition to special muzzleloading seasons, most states and provinces also allow muzzleloaders to be used during their regular rifle and/or shotgun seasons. Most muzzleloading rifles have always offered better hunting accuracy than the average slug-shooting smoothbore shotgun. The bottom line on hunting with an in-line muzzleloader will always be this: "You only get one shot, but it's a good shot." This will always be true if you take the time to learn

how to harness the full potential of your in-line rifle. Even then, however, let's not kid ourselves: While muzzleloading is a special sport, it's best viewed as "taking a step backwards" and doing things differently from the centerfire crowd. If you don't make your one shot count, it's highly unlikely you can redeem yourself on the same deer.

Here is an example of how our muzzleloading group did things differently.

My son and I belong to an "exclusive" group of in-line hunters nicknamed "The Mid-Morning Outfitters." We consider ourselves exclusive because not many folks would tolerate the "roughing-it" style of camping that goes on during our outings. On one of our most memorable hunts, my buddy "Chopper" led us to a favored hunting area in southeastern Saskatchewan. We made camp in a small aspen bluff on land that we had permission to hunt. This job involves erecting a tent that can accommodate 20 people, maybe more.

Chopper likes to do things on a large scale. Unfortunately, he tends to forget small details like rope, chimney sections, foam mattresses and black

What's the bottom line on hunting whitetails with an in-line? You only get one shot, but it's a good shot.

powder. Saskatchewan does not allow hunting on Sundays, which is a good thing when my buddies are putting up camp. If we're lucky, we can set up the tent in one day. Several hours after starting the job — including a couple of trips to the nearest town to purchase rope and chimney pipe for our new home-made furnace — our camp was ready. The tent was comfortable, complete with a foot-thick straw sleeping area to replace the forgotten mattresses. And while these guys are all former game wardens from the far north, and pride themselves on being "bush-apes," they're better deer hunters than they are campers.

We scouted for deer during the last hour of light that first day, and saw dozens of animals within walking distance of camp. We were in whitetail heaven. Each hunter selected a spot for the morning hunt. We decided to start the hunt by watching fields and trails, and then hang tree stands at midday after learning more about the deer's movement patterns. Our Knight MK-85s were sighted in and ready.

That evening we watched intently as Chopper "pressure-cooked" several unopened cans of stew

and beans in his huge wood furnace. This was a "Northern" trick, whereby you stare at all of the cans, watching for a seam to start bulging. When a can started to grow, our chef quickly grabbed it from the fire with a large pair of pliers before it blew up. Not being "Northerners," my son, Glen, and I couldn't bear to watch this procedure. We were convinced the tent was about to be wallpapered with beans and stew. Amazingly, the method worked, probably saving three or four minutes from the more conventional method of heating with pots, but with much more excitement.

The next morning we hunted, and no one saw any deer. Not one animal! We found excellent sign everywhere, but no critters fed or moved. That afternoon we tried our spots again and were rewarded with dozens of opportunities, and each hunter shot a doe for the freezer. Some of us hunted from tree stands, while others hunkered in ground-blinds. We all used

Despite the in-line's popularity, hunter numbers during special muzzleloading deer seasons remain modest when compared to participants in regular firearms and, in some cases, archery seasons.

The author's in-line hunting partners, pictured above, call themselves the Mid-Morning Outfitters. They enjoy roughing it in a tent camp during Saskatchewan's muzzleloading deer season.

Flambeau deer decoys, both Redi-does and feeding does, with great success. We saw some good bucks, but did not get shots at any antlered deer. Because we each had three tags, good for a buck and two does, we were having a great time.

The next morning was a repeat of the first, no deer. That afternoon, we saw many animals and again filled more tags. Chopper killed a fine buck, his first big buck with his muzzleloader. When the alarm rang the next morning, no one budged. After a brief discussion — very brief — we decided that hunting was much better in the afternoon, so we all went back to sleep. It felt strange lying inside a warm sleeping bag inside a freezing tent as the sun slowly lighted the sky during a deer hunt.

We had another good hunt that afternoon, and only one day remained. Needless to say, we slept in

again, waiting until Mother Nature called each hunter from his warm bag. The first person up had to build a fire, which cut the chill from the air inside the huge tent. That afternoon, we all filled our tags and took down the tent, using the headlights of our vehicles to illuminate the campsite.

We then shook hands and vowed to reconvene our "Mid-Morning Outfitters" group the next year. The hunt made for many great memories, none of which would have happened if not for the province's muzzleloading season and the allure of hunting with in-line rifles.

CHAPTER 2

Developing and Manufacturing In-Line Muzzleloaders

While most muzzleloading hunters in the 1980s were happy with their traditional barrel-stuffers, they weren't in love. They were primarily interested in hunting, not making smoke. As a result, many of them jumped at the chance to shoot and hunt with muzzleloading rifles that more closely resembled their reliable centerfire rifles in looks and function.

The history of the modern in-line muzzle-loading rifle is short compared to many other firearms used by today's hunters. In-line rifles — as we know them — date back to 1983 when a group of Missouri hunters complained to a gunsmith about the poor performance of their traditional muzzleloaders. They had gone to Colorado to take part in a muzzleloader season for elk. During their hunt, they were continually disappointed in their rifle's accuracy and reliability. Tony Knight, proprietor of the Knight Gun and Archery Shop near Lancaster, Mo., listened to their complaints and decided he could come up with a more reliable muzzleloader. Knight worked on some designs that showed promise, and the next year some of his prototypes proved successful during the hunters' Colorado elk hunt.

The Rebirth of In-Lines

Back in the 1980s, most muzzleloading hobbyists were primarily target shooters. Companies such as Lyman, Thompson/Center Arms, Connecticut Valley Arms, and Hatfield supplied long-barreled sidehammers that were used in black-powder competitions and target shoots. Most shooters complemented the traditional-styled long rifles with tomahawks, Bowie knives, shaggy beards and homemade buckskin clothes. Perhaps surprisingly, many of these hobbyists loved target shooting with their smokepoles, but hunting was not an important pastime for them. Of

Modern Muzzleloading Photo

Tony Knight, above, wanted a more consistent-firing muzzleloader for hunting. This led him to reinvent an old concept — the in-line ignition. The term "in-line" refers to the ignition flame's position behind or in line with the combustion chamber. This "injects" the ignition flame directly into the chamber, resulting in a more reliable ignition than the angled flame path of a traditional muzzleloader.

course, not everyone owning a black-powder rifle felt this way. These hunters lobbied wildlife agencies for special hunting seasons, hence the advent of primitive weapon seasons. These hunts soon became designated as muzzleloader seasons.

Although most traditional muzzleloading enthusiasts were set in their ways, some looked for better, more consistent results from their hunting rifles. When Knight dispensed with the sidehammer and designed modern-looking rifles with straight-pull cocking handles, double safeties and in-line ignitions, many hunters realized the benefits and asked for his new muzzleloaders.

From a meager five or six prototypes, Knight

learned enough about building in-lines to put together a "production run" of 25 rifles. He took these rifles to Indiana and sold them to gunshops, where they were quickly snapped up by deer hunters. Knight soon saw the potential of his in-line designs, and was impressed with the demand for his rifles.

He then spelled out three objectives. First, his in-line rifles must be inherently safe firearms. He ensured this by designing a foolproof double safety system. One safety was a knurled nut that spun along the threaded hammer stem. Spinning the nut forward prevented the hammer from making a complete forward motion to strike the capped nipple. The second safety was a more traditional block of the trigger mechanism, preventing the trigger from moving and releasing the sear.

Second, Knight wanted a reliable rifle. He kept his designs simple and strong. He believes "injecting" the ignition flame straight into the combustion chamber provides more reliable ignition than the angled flame path of traditional muzzleloaders.

Third, he demanded the best accuracy possible.

Modern Muzzleloading Photo

Knight experimented with barrel twists, lengths and barrel-makers. As his research and development progressed, the new rifles consistently exceeded his accuracy expectations.

Del Ramsay's Sabots

At about the same time Knight was working on his early in-line designs, he heard about an Arkansas shooter named Del Ramsay who was developing the saboted bullet concept. Knight had also conceived a saboted bullet, but he simply did not have the time to perfect his bullet ideas. Del's designs were spurred by this unhappy fact: His big conical muzzleloading bullets frequently didn't knock down whitetails as well as he expected. He wondered why his .44 Magnum killed whitetails more quickly than his muzzleloader's heavy slugs. After much experimenting, he devised a successful method for shooting handgun bullets in his black-powder rifles.

Ramsay's sabots were simply plastic sleeved-cups into which he inserted pistol bullets. The sabots had bore diameters for .50- and .54-caliber muzzleloaders, and they could be dyed different colors to desig-

Arkansas hunter and shooter Del Ramsay was unhappy with the performance of heavy conical muzzleloading bullets on white-tailed deer. He believed a smaller projectile would perform better. This led him to develop a plastic-sleeved cup, or sabot, to hold .38-caliber and .44-caliber pistol bullets. The sabot provides a gas seal, imprints into the rifling, and carries the bullet down the bore. The sabot falls away after leaving the barrel.

nate their bore specs. The sabots had a hollow base that "upset," or flattened, upon ignition to ensure a good gas seal. By varying the thickness of the sabot's petals, different bullet sizes could be shimmed for use in much larger bores. This enabled shooters to fire .38- or .44-caliber pistol bullets in a standard .50-caliber rifle.

The smooth, slippery plastic used in sabots allowed easy, consistent loading down any proper sized bore. In addition, the plastic did not melt or coat the bore, as some early experimenters feared. As Ramsay refined his production techniques, sabots continued to improve the accuracy of in-line muzzleloaders. Ramsay's new sabots were a perfect match

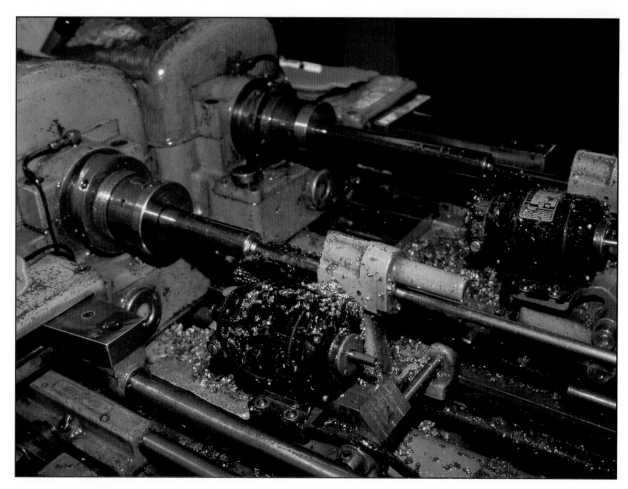

Muzzleloading rifle barrels are first cut to length and straightened before going through the drilling and reaming process. The gun-drill, similar to a lathe, uses a carbide cutter to drill the barrel within a few thousandths of an inch. Reaming the barrel, above, enlarges the bore to the final dimensions and leaves it mirror smooth.

for Knight's in-line rifles, and they took the market by storm.

Those sabot designs are probably one of the shooting industry's most taken-for-granted components. Why? Probably because they're little and they work so well that they seldom draw attention to themselves.

The Heart of the In-Line

As Knight continued producing his rifles, he soon determined that the barrel is the muzzleloader's heart. He purchased barrels from suppliers in Montana and Germany that made them with the faster-twist rifling specified. He soon learned that a one-turn-in-28-inches twist was the best performer for in-line rifles. His research was proven correct over time, and the 1-in-28 twist was adopted by virtu-

ally all of his competitors.

Demand continued to build, and Knight struggled to build enough of his rifles to fill the orders and maintain his gun-shop business. He also continued to work with Ramsay to perfect the "shootability" of saboted bullets. Even though neither man could know it for certain, the in-line rifle was on its way to fame and fortune.

Knight's Big Decision

As demand for the Knight Rifle exploded, Knight had to make a big decision. He shut down his gun and archery shop and concentrated on manufacturing in-line muzzleloaders. He obtained enough money to build an 8,000-square-foot factory in Lancaster, Mo., and then started building Knight in-line muzzleloaders in quantity. Although he contracted out much of the actual fabrication, he assembled the parts in his new facility. The business prospered. Several years later he moved to a new, larger location in Centerville, Iowa, about 30 miles from his original factory. Many of his original employees commuted to the new facility, and rifle production continued to expand.

As Knight tried to meet the hunting public's ever-increasing demand for his rifles, the life of an industrialist took its toll. Although business was incredibly strong, Knight found he had less time to do the things at which he excelled. The work demands also forced him to spend too much time doing things he did not enjoy. Knight is a hunter, an inventor and gun-builder. He never really enjoyed the business demands of operating his own company. In 1990, he sold the operation to the Dale Watley family. Knight stayed with the company to promote in-line muzzleloaders in his own special way and to do the research-and-development work he loved.

Under Watley's ownership, Knight Rifles — also known as Modern Muzzleloading — experienced phenomenal growth and success. With Knight's continual input, the company's product line widened and innovative new materials were incorporated into the muzzleloaders. These innovations included stainless steel, composite stocks, Monte Carlo stocks, "dipped" camo coverings and fiber-optics sights.

As the in-line revolution progressed in the early 1990s, many other companies rushed rifles onto the market. Connecticut Valley Arms was the first company to join the race, but it was with the company's ill-fated Apollo in-line. (The Apollo was recalled and replaced a few years after it came onto the market.) The design of many of these new entries appeared to be trying to capitalize on groundwork laid by Knight and Ramsay during the 1980s.

Muzzleloading rifle barrels are rifled using one of two methods. "Cut rifling" scratches away metal with a cutting tool and leaves a deep groove preferred by traditional shooters who shoot patched round-balls. "Button rifling" impresses a groove into the metal using a hardened "button."

The Basic Design

The in-line muzzleloader is a relatively simple firearm. Its basics included an action, a barrel, stock, sights, ramrod, bolt (also called a striker, hammer or cocking-piece), nipple, breech plug and trigger assembly. All in-lines have these base components. Of course, manufacturers design these parts using many variations. That's how we get such an assortment of choices in the gun racks.

Let's examine the in-line's key parts. Although they're of myriad designs, the basic function of each part is the same. The most successful muzzleloader designs are based on simplicity. The fewer parts the

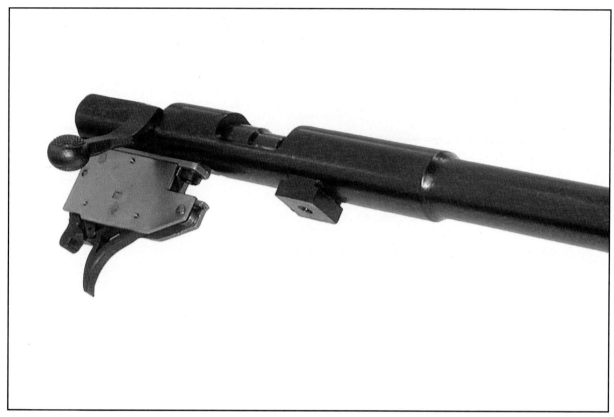

Many of today's in-lines have a one-piece barreled action. Machining the barrel and action into a single unit is stronger and less expensive than manufacturing the barrel and action separately. The barreled action above is the CVA Mono-Block.

better. The primary reason for that consideration is the inherently dirty nature of combustion in these rifles, whether with black powder or its substitutes. Residues — both sooty and granular — are left throughout the barrel and action, and on accessories such as scopes and ramrods. These residues are messy and prone to causing rust. More about that later.

Building a Barrel

Let's review these key parts by starting with the barrel, the heart of the in-line muzzleloader. In-line rifle barrels are manufactured using the same procedures employed when making centerfire rifle barrels. Some even use the same steel. The art of rifle-barrel making has not changed significantly for years. It is practiced expertly at the Green Mountain Barrels and T/C factory in New Hampshire, both of which employ a fascinating blend of machining and hand-workmanship.

In-line barrels start as 12- to 16-foot steel rods varying in thickness from ⅞-inch to 2 inches. The rods are precision-cut to an overall length, and then

started on an engineering sequence that turns them into tight-shooting muzzleloading barrels. First the freshly cut-off blanks are straightened, which ensures the deep-hole drills will run down the blank's exact center. Most blanks are straightened two or three times while being converted to barrels. The machinists, using simple jigs that indicate misalignments, skillfully apply pressure with large jacks until each heavy steel blank spins true.

The prospective barrel is next placed into a large, deep-hole drilling machine. Looking somewhat like a huge lathe, the drilling machine holds two barrels. The machine spins the barrels at fairly high speed, varying from 2,500 rpm to 4,000 rpm, and then moves the barrels slowly toward a long gun-drill. The gun-drill is a hollow steel rod with a super-tough carbide cutter silver-soldered on its end. The cutter is just a few-thousandths of an inch less than the desired bore size. As the spinning blank contacts the cutter and the hole starts, oil pumps under high pressure into the rod to lubricate the cutting head and wash away the cut chips. The oil and chips are caught for recycling. The barrel advances about one to four inches per minute, depending on the type of steel.

After being drilled, the barrel is taken to the reaming department, where the hole is precisely smoothed. The barrel is held stationary and an oil-cooled spinning reamer, somewhat similar to the

deep-hole drill, removes a few-thousandths of an inch, enlarging the hole and leaving it mirror-smooth. Reaming is a critical operation. The final dimensions it produces influence how well a barrel shoots.

After reaming, the barrels go to the rifling department, where rifling is cut or impressed into the length of the bore. Cut rifling is the original method of creating barrels, and button rifling is a newer process that significantly speeds up production. These two methods, along with hammer-forging, are the methods employed worldwide to produce rifle barrels. Hammer-forging, a process that uses incredible force to squeeze rifling into the barrel, is not used for making in-line barrels.

Cut rifling is still preferred by traditional shooters, because the deeper grooves work best with patched round-balls. The shallower button rifling works great with sabots and conical bullets. Cut rifling takes longer, averaging more than 15 minutes to create a rifled barrel. Button rifling requires about one minute per barrel.

Barrel straightness is essential to accuracy. Barrel blanks are precision-straightened before drilling, and checked for straightness throughout the milling process. Air gauging, shown above, is considered the most precise way to measure a barrel's straightness.

Cut rifling involves "scratching" away metal with a small square cutting tool, which looks like a hook projecting near the end of a long, hollow rod. The "hook" is the width of the groove and is adjustable for depth. Precision machinery moves the cutting hook back and forth in exactly the correct starting locations to cut whatever number of grooves are desired. The barrel is automatically indexed for each pass, and the cutter is automatically adjusted for depth.

The button-rifling process is much easier and quicker. Essentially, a hardened button containing the reverse image of the lands grooves is dragged or pushed from one end of the barrel to the other. This results in the barrel elongating and widening slightly

After the barrel's finish is applied, sights, triggers, stocks and other parts are assembled. Above, workers at Thompson/Center Arms assemble the Black Diamond in-line rifle.

uing along the production path.

After a check for straightness, and precision bending to ensure the barrel is straight, the barrel's external dimensions are machined. Special tracer-lathes follow a "master" as they cut away the outer steel to desired dimensions. The barrel is next rechecked for straightness and final length, and then a crown is precisely machined into one end. If the barrel is to be used for an in-line rifle with an integral action, its overall length will include the necessary inches for reaming out the action. The barrel is placed into a CNC machine, essentially a robotic milling device that takes its orders from computer programs. Once in the CNC machine, the action and trigger cut-outs are precisely milled. In addition, any profiling and necessary holes, flats or grooves are drilled or machined. Every task is done exactly the same, time after time, with extreme precision.

After the barrel, or barreled-action, is completed, skilled assemblers tap sight holes, and the manufacturer's identification and the rifle's serial number are roll-stamped into the barrel. This is usually the step where chrome-moly barreled actions or semi-finished barrels are blued. Stainless steel muzzleloader barrels, however, are bead-blasted to an even sheen instead of being blued.

After the finish is applied, the barreled action becomes a "part," and it is taken to installers who add other parts to

because of the displacement of metal. A special smoothing button might also be passed through to ensure a perfect finish to the bore. All of this cutting and metal-displacement can create internal stresses in the barrel. These stresses can be relieved by a combination of intense heat and proper cooling. Most barrels, particularly the button-rifled types, are therefore stress-relieved in large ovens before contin-

create a finished rifle. Sights, triggers, cocking-handles, stocks and all the parts that create an in-line are adeptly put together in order. Assemblers can put together up to 25 rifles per hour. After the complete barreled action is tightened into its stock and the sights are aligned, the ramrod is slid into place, and the rifle gets a final inspection and polish before going to final packaging.

Design of the In-Line's Actions

The in-line's action is the one component that varies the most significantly in design between rifle models. Basically, there are two designs of in-line actions: the integral barrel/action and the centerfire-type action, which is a separate unit from the barrel. In many in-line rifles, the action is threaded to receive the barrel's shank, which is similar to the barreled actions on most centerfire rifles.

Most actions, however, are simple steel tubes with a threaded end and cutouts for the trigger and breech. Many in-line actions differ from centerfire designs because they do not need significant recoil lugs. Some actions are contoured for a unique shape, but most are round in profile. At Modern Muzzleloading, Knight originally preferred an octagon shape for his actions. That design preference changed in time, however, and now most actions are round because it's simpler and cheaper.

The simple one-piece barreled action has come to dominate the design of most successful in-line rifles. By incorporating the barrel and action into a single unit, the rifle should be inherently stronger while cutting manufacturing costs.

In-Line Triggers

The trigger assemblies of many in-lines frequently emulate successful centerfire rifle designs. Most triggers attach to the receiver with one or two large bolts, and they usually incorporate an integral safety mechanism that locks the trigger. In-line triggers are single-stage units that usually come factory-set at about 3 to 8 pounds. The optimum trigger setting varies by individual, but most longtime shooters prefer a trigger weight of 2½ to 4 pounds for hunting. The trigger pull should be crisp, which means it

Skilled assemblers can complete 25 rifles in an hour. Above, workers at Millennium Designed Muzzleloaders assemble the Buck-Waka and M2K.

should break cleanly without excessive movement before and after release. Most in-line triggers can be adjusted for pull weight. Most can also be adjusted for "creep," movement before release; and slop, movement after release. Most factories prefer or demand that such adjustments be carried out by a qualified gunsmith.

Today's in-lines feature the same stock materials and innovations found in centerfire rifles. Many feature high combs, making it easier for hunters to use a scope. Synthetic materials are growing in popularity, largely because hunters demand durable, maintenance-free hunting arms. In addition, synthetic stocks often feature the latest camouflage patterns, making them even more attractive to hunters.

The most common type of in-line firing mechanism uses a cocking handle on the side or on the back of the action. The in-line above is the Knight MK-95.

Rifle Stocks for In-Lines

Stock design and material closely follow trends set by centerfire rifles. High combs that align the shooter's eye to the scope are common, and composite stocks have replaced wood in popularity. Many manufacturers offer a choice of camouflage patterns for the stocks, and competition in the marketplace ensures the most current camo patterns are featured. Many companies offer thumb-hole stocks on their in-lines, particularly as an option on the most expensive models. Thumb-holes are fast handling stocks that place the shooter's eye directly behind a scope. Shooters love them or hate them, because this is purely a matter of choice. One consideration regarding thumb-holes: They don't work for left-handed shooters, because the prominent cheek-piece makes cheek-weld uncomfortable. Although several left-hand thumbholes have been offered, it appears they are not an important issue with manufacturers.

One major difference between in-line muzzleloaders and centerfire rifles is bedding. Centerfire rifles employ several bedding techniques to ensure the action is securely and uniformly seated into the stock. Various bedding compounds that create a perfectly molded fit are used, hence the term glass-bedding. Strangely, muzzleloader manufacturers have not yet adopted this degree of precision. In-lines shoot very well as-is, but accuracy can be improved by bedding the action into the stock.

Ramrods are also a key component of in-line muzzleloaders. Until recently, most ramrods were made from straight-grained hardwood dowels with brass end attachments. Fiberglass rods virtually replaced the wooden ones, and now solid or hollow aluminum rods are dominating the market. Ramrods must be held securely in place, and they should not make any rattling or similar sounds.

The Breech Plug

In-line muzzleloading rifles can be divided into two categories: those with a sealed breech and those with removable breech plugs. In reality, all in-lines and traditional rifles — whether percussion or flintlock — have breech plugs. That's because barrels are drilled all the way through when they're manufactured. Sealed-breech styles are plugged and perma-

Bolt-action in-lines are popular, largely because they resemble the fit, feel and operation of bolt-action centerfire rifles. The in-line rifle shown above is the Remington 700ML.

nently sealed with a weld. They should not to be removed by the owner.

In-Line Nipples

The nipple on a muzzleloader holds the ignition device: either a musket cap or a No. 11 percussion cap. When the hammer strikes the cap to ignite it, a flame bursts through a small hole in the nipple and through the breech plug to the propellant. The nipple's outer shape and dimensions are important to ensure the cap has a tight friction fit. The nipple must also serve as a seal to prevent excessive gas blow-back as the detonation blasts the bullet down the bore. The No. 11 percussion caps fit tighter than do the "newer" musket caps, which have a series of splits around their outer edge.

In recent years, innovative nipple designs have been designed to provide better ignition than did original nipples. The Knight Red Hot and T/C's Flame

Thrower nipples are examples of newer, more innovative technology. In-line hunters should replace worn nipples when caps do not fit securely or when accuracy starts to deteriorate. Nipples wear out. They must be replaced just like spark plugs in automobiles.

Firing Mechanisms for In-Lines

In-line muzzleloaders can be separated into four basic types by action design, and how the bolt or hammer is cocked for firing. What follows is a brief description of each style.

First, some models use a cocking handle on one side, or a striker that is pulled back to cock the action. These models are a basic design that is offered by all major manufacturers. Specifically, this list includes past and current companies, including Knight Rifles, T/C, Traditions, CVA, Marlin, Lyman, White, Gonic, Navy Arms, Cabela's, Bass Pro Shops, Millennium Designed Muzzleloaders and a few others.

The second type of in-line is the bolt-action. Some of these are based on existing centerfire actions, but others are entirely new designs. Bolt-actions are this

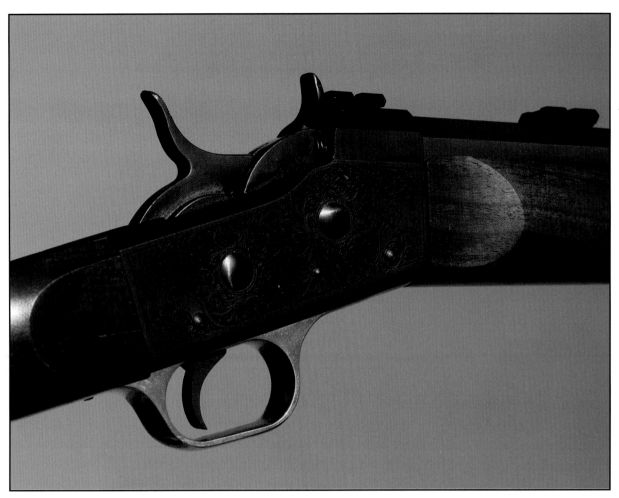

Some in-lines use a hammer-type action similar to that of the Winchester Model 94. The in-line above is Cabela's Rolling Block.

market's "hot" design, usually touted for delivering maximum accuracy and performance. Bolt-action designs are offered by Knight Rifles, Remington, Traditions, CVA, Ruger, and Austin & Halleck.

The third type of in-line action is considered the traditional in-line design. It borrows from older firearms designs, such as the Winchester Model 94 and Remington rolling block. This category includes rifles from T/C (Scout), Kahnke, Markesbery, Cabela's and Pedesoli.

The fourth type of in-line actions are unique designs that don't fit any of the above categories. These rifles are stand-alone designs, although every new model will likely be copied at some point. Examples of these "miscellaneous" styles are the Prairie River Arms bullpup, the discontinued Piefer TS-93, and the break-open T/C Encore and Millennium Designed Muzzleloader's Buck-Waka.

So Many Choices

In-line hunters have never had such an array of choices. In-line rifles are being sold in price-points or dollar-value-ranges, that create extreme competition among manufacturers. The marketplace determines

which models survive as manufacturers steadily improve their products and introduce new models. Quality and value are major factors, of course. Many shooters who bought entry-level in-lines or earlier models will upgrade to what they perceive to be higher-performance models. Many in-line shooters are comfortable owning more than one in-line rifle. This allows them to share the sport with their children and friends. I'm aware of several friends who keep their "old" in-lines for use as loaners after they buy newer models. Some hunters have scoped and unscoped in-lines so they can more conveniently hunt states with differing laws for sights.

Learning a Lesson

With the mention of owning multiple in-line rifles, I'm reminded of another Mid-Morning Outfitter incident. We were hunting in an area that had serious crop-damage problems, so we were given several doe tags in addition to our one buck tag. With all

these extra tags, we decided this was a great opportunity to test muzzleloading bullets while taking surplus deer to donate to the local food-bank. Deer seemed to be everywhere, and our hunt was proceeding relatively smoothly. Despite a few missed shots, we each shot one or two deer every evening as we hunted from 3 p.m. or 4 p.m. until shooting hours ended.

Our tree stands overlooked heavily used deer trails, and we frequently had opportunities to shoot more than one deer at a time. During one of these times when I was surrounded by deer, I devised a great plan. I had brought along a T/C Firehawk and a Knight Wolverine, and had planned to hunt with them on alternating days. But because there were so many deer and we had so many tags, I pondered whether to take both to my stand.

The more that I thought about it, the better I liked the idea of being an equal-opportunity in-line hunter. After I climbed into my ladder stand, my son helped me secure each rifle before going his separate way. My plan worked great. I always had a ready rifle, and I killed more deer that evening than what might have been possible with only one rifle. We were soon busy skinning and taking venison to the food-bank's freezer-trailer.

Unfortunately, a problem arose. The next after-

Although many of today's in-line rifles share common designs, new concepts are being developed every year. The in-line above, the Markesbery Black Bear, is based on a design developed by independent riflemaker Gordon Kahnke of Minnesota.

noon, a group of deer came down the trail. I brought one of the rifles to bear, and slowly squeezed off the shot. Misfire! I recocked the rifle and tried again. Still no shot! No problem. I put down the rifle on the padded armrest and brought the other in-line into position. Misfire! I tried again with the same results.

What was the likelihood of having two in-line rifles malfunction at the same time? What was going on? The caps were going off, but I had no ignition. Then it hit me. In all my excitement and anticipation of being a venison-getting machine with two rifles, I had forgotten to reload them! I guess toting two rifles was too complicated for me, so I went back to hunting with one in-line rifle at a time.

Hunters today have an array of in-line designs and price ranges to choose from. As in-line hunters become more serious about muzzleloading, they often upgrade from entry-level rifles to more expensive models they believe will perform better. But do they? In Chapter 4, the author compares and rates today's in-line rifles.

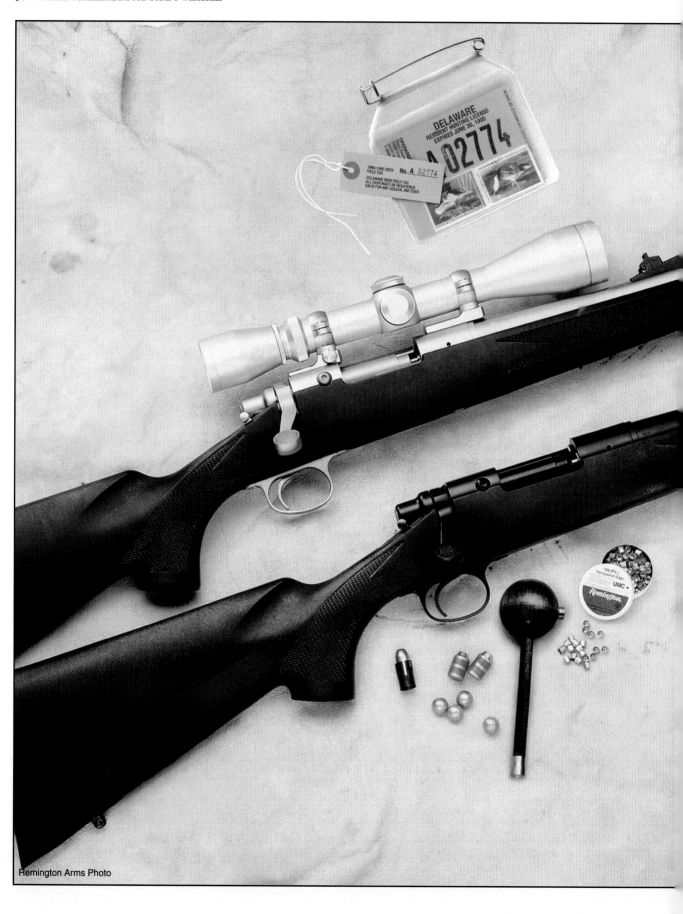

Remington Arms Photo

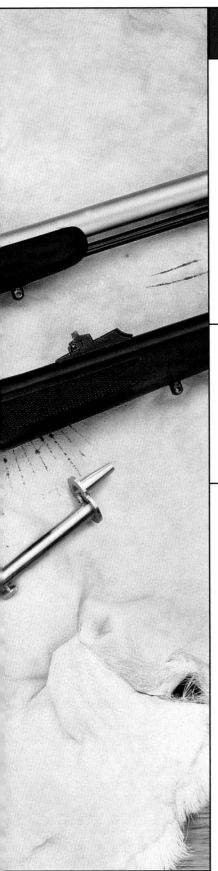

Today's In-Line Muzzleloaders

During the 1990s, in-line rifles went from a curiosity to the dominant force in muzzleloading deer hunting. Sometimes controversial and sometimes scorned, the in-line prevailed with hunters who are more interested in reliable performance than re-creating history.

In-line rifles were the big muzzleloading news of the 1990s, and their popularity was holding strong as deer hunters stalked into the new millennium. In less than two decades, the in-line became a significant hunting rifle throughout the United States and Canada.

Many industry experts said the in-line came of age when the Remington Arms Co. entered the market in 1996. Other big names like Ruger and Marlin followed suit, attesting to the significance of the "in-line revolution." Given time, most deer hunters will associate the in-line design with the terms "muzzleloader" or "black-powder rifle" as the traditionally styled sidehammer rifles fade away.

The muzzleloading world has never been the same since Tony Knight crafted his first in-line rifles, and started selling and promoting their reliable design. Some proponents of Knight's concept say the timing was right, that hunters were ready for a new tool because they did not want the hassle that accompanied traditional muzzleloaders. Traditionalists, of course, consider the new design too slick, too modern, to be included in the "primitive-weapons" hunts they had fought for.

Shaking Up and Breaking Tradition

Technically, however, the straight-line ignition concept goes back to the 1700s. The question, however, is if anyone really cares. Most deer hunters don't

Hunters seek safety and performance from an in-line. Many in-line rifles, such as the Knight DISC rifle, above, feature a centerfire-style safety behind the bolt, and a screw-action safety on the cocking knob. The red ring indicates the cocking knob is in the firing postion.

care much about such history. Why? They're having too much fun to worry about the ancestry of their rifles. Besides, the ancestry of most in-lines being shot in the year 2000 can be measured in months and years, not the decades and centuries that flintlocks and side-locks went through in their evolution.

Without exaggeration, the in-line rifle has been at the heart of more sophisticated research and product development in the past decade than what transpired in the many centuries before, dating back to when man first ignited black powder.

As I watched the evolution of the in-line industry in the 1990s, I could not help but draw a parallel with the snowmobile industry. When snowmobiling skyrocketed in popularity in the 1960s, the number of companies in

the market was well into the 20s or low 30s. Everyone got into the act, even major farm-machinery companies such as John Deere and Massey-Fergusson. With time, the market flattened and many companies withdrew, leaving a handful of brands that continue to dominate the sport. Interestingly, most of the survivors were the originators, the first into the market. In recent years, that same process is occurring with in-line muzzleloaders.

Everyone has heard the old saying about the cream rising to the top, and this happened quickly with in-line muzzleloaders. Manufacturers with the best designs were maintaining or gaining market-share as the 1900s ended. Many brands and models were dropping, including some well-built rifles that entered the market with great fanfare but no staying power. The dropouts were usually overpriced or simply inferior products when compared to standards being set by the more successful companies.

Many manufacturers of black-powder rifles today are sharing basic ideas on what hunters

want. Stainless steel is perceived as exciting and alluring, as are camo-composite stocks with straight combs or cheek-pieces designed for scope shooters. All of the in-lines have fast-twist barrels for shooting saboted bullets. Most in-lines have high-quality adjustable triggers and many have two safeties. Their barrels are generally 24 inches long, having dropped from "shotgun length" down to "hunting rifle length." Specifically, the long 30-inch tubes were replaced by 22- to 24-inch barrels. No doubt, some of the rifles with 26-inch barrels will be touted as adding significant "performance," but I find the longer barrels make these rifles a bit more clumsy to handle in the field.

The bottom line is that the most successful models are inherently accurate, easy to maintain, and handle much like popular centerfire rifles. This makes the transition relatively easy for shooters who are experienced with most deer rifles. They don't need to worry about hooked buttplates made of brass, and drooping stocks designed for aligning open sights.

Today's in-lines feature shorter barrels than the long barrels popular among traditional muzzleloading designs. Most in-line barrels are 22 to 24 inches long. Some companies offer 26-inch barrels, but the author finds longer barrels are more awkward in the field.

Open sights, of course, also underwent significant modernization, with crude "partridge-style" rear sights giving way to hi-tech fiber-optic units that pick up available light and glow in contrasting colors. The use of green dots on each side of the rear-sight notch and a contrasting red dot on the front-sight blade makes for remarkably fast and accurate sight alignment.

The In-Line's Breech Plugs

That brings us to a piece of the in-line rifle that was developed for these firearms: the removable breech plug. Like it or not, the removable breech plug has prevailed in the marketplace, and all in-lines today use that design.

Lets examine each type of breech-plug

The removable breech plug is a stainless steel plug that threads into the rear end of the barrel. It is clearly visible on the Thompson/Center Arms 209x50 Encore at left. The breech plug, above left, has a threaded hole on one end to accompany the nipple, above right. The ensemble directs the ignition flame to the propellant in the firing chamber.

design in greater depth.

The Fixed Breech-Plug Design

Some in-line muzzleloader designs have threaded plugs that — more or less — are permanently installed fixtures that seal one end of the barrel, forming a breech. Some examples of this design include the discontinued T/C Thunderhawks and Firehawks. These breech plugs screw into the barrel and conform to its external dimensions to form a smooth "end" or receiver portion. Somewhere on the outside face of the permanent plug, usually in the exact center, is a threaded hole

that will accept a nipple. This forms the passage that allows the flame to ignite the powder charge. The nonremovable breech plugs lost the popularity contest, but for no compelling reason. Only a couple of rifles still employ this design, which is unfortunate. Some of the best shooting and most easily maintained muzzleloaders used this design.

The Removable Breech-Plug Design

The removable breech plug is a stainless steel plug that threads into the rear end of the barrel, usually stopping flush with the breech's end. Removable breech plugs usually have a standard-sized threaded hole in one end for the nipple, and a hollowed out body on the other end, where the ignition flames hit the charge. Removable breech plugs are a key element in the ignition system, and manufacturers have employed a bewildering range of designs. Originally, some removable breech

The Knight rifles pictured above are the DISC, top; the MK-85, middle; and the T-Bolt, bottom.

plugs even had integral nipples, but these fell out of use fairly quickly.

Common sense would dictate that the shorter the breech plug opening ahead of the nipple, the shorter the distance flames must travel to the powder charge. This fact does not seem to be universally accepted, because some breech plugs are much longer than others. Why? Breech plugs must have enough length and enough threads to ensure the plug can withstand the pressures generated by ignition and detonation of the powder charge.

Some manufacturers believe breech plugs can affect accuracy, and have experimented with designs that improved ignition. Despite such improvements, I'm still skeptical that removable breech plugs are as convenient and necessary as many shooters believe. They're a major source of problems in muzzleloader maintenance. When they're improperly lubricated and overtightened, they can become virtually welded into the barrel. And although cleaning your in-line "just like a shotgun barrel" is handy when the breech plug is out, I've never really had problems cleaning black-powder rifles with sealed breeches. I suspect the higher pressures involved in containing the 150-grain loads suggested for many new in-lines worsens maintenance problems. Nipples and breech plugs should be well-lubed and finger-tightened only.

Variables with In-Lines

Now that we've discussed the in-line rifle's main features, let's delve deeper into some of the variables you will encounter with these guns. After all, "variables" are critical in muzzleloading. You must become adept at understanding and controlling them.

Sabots, lubes, sights, powder types, powder

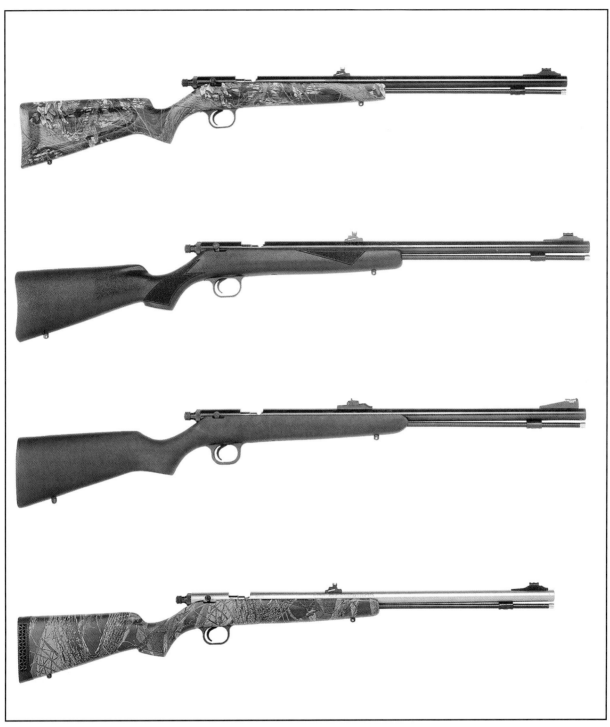

charges, bullet styles, cleaning procedures, seating pressure, patch material, barrel twists, sighting-in distances and other details are all part of this game. The biggest decision prospective muzzleloaders face, however, is determining which rifle to buy. This decision is the starting point from which all other variables burst forth and multiply. Selecting a muzzleloading rifle usually involves finding a model

The Modern Muzzleloading Knight rifles in-lines pictured above are, from top, the Wolverine, Wolverine II, American Knight and Bighorn.

that looks and feels good. Naturally, the rifle must also fit your pocketbook. We also expect reasonable accuracy, although most new owners expect they'll have to hone some skills to obtain good results. Having helped

Thompson/Center Arms has a reputation for producing well-designed in-line muzzleloading rifles. Shown here are the 209x50 Encore, top, and the Black Diamond.

many people choose new muzzleloaders, I've learned a few things about comparing the many different in-lines available.

Unfortunately, this job is never easy because the in-line market is in constant flux. Innovations, stiff competition and technological advances spur the development of new or revamped models. At times it even appears new rifles are squeezing out the current offerings on gun-shop shelves.

Rather than trying to discuss every possible in-line you could consider, let's look primarily at rifles from the "Big-4" manufacturers and a couple of relative newcomers that are holding their own. We'll also look at some older or discontinued models that offer hunters an interesting in-line option in the used-gun marketplace.

In Chapter 4, we'll examine most of these rifles in greater depth, so what follows is a brief overview of manufacturers and key models that were introduced in the year 2000.

The Knight Rifle

Tony Knight continues to design innovative in-lines for the Modern Muzzle Loading Co. Here is a look at some of his rifle designs:

✓The MK-85 is the original in-line Knight rifle, and remains the workhorse of the line. It's available in many variations.

✓ The BK-92 was an economy model of the MK-85

✓ The T-5 was an economy, bare-bones version of the MK-85 that used foreign-made parts.

✓ The LK-93 can be found in the Wolverine, American Knight, Big Horn and Legend rifle lines. This model features a trimmer, simpler design that is also available in several stocks and steel.

✓ The MK-95 used magnum rifle primers for ignition in a miniature bolt-action design.

✓ The DISC, or Dual Ignition System Concept, rifle is a modern bolt-action design that uses percussion caps or No. 209 shotshell primers to ignite up to 150 grains of powder.

✓ The T-BOLT is a straight pull-action design that partially encloses the nipple.

✓ The .45 Super will set a new standard for in-line performance.

Thompson/Center Arms

T/C makes muzzleloaders that combine sound design, excellent materials and beautifully consistent workmanship.

✓ The T/C Scout is a traditional design that looks like a Model 94 Winchester with no lever. "Carbine" best describes the Scout.

✓ The T/C Thunderhawk and Firehawk are discontinued designs with side-cocking handles and a variety of choices in stocks and steel. Both are excellent shooters that just plain work great.

✓ The T/C System 1 rifles looked like oversized Firehawks. Closer examination, however, shows a detachable 26-inch barrel and removable breech plug.

✓ The T/C 209x50 Encore rifles are probably the most versatile firearm on the market

The Traditions rifles pictured above are the Lightning Bolt, top; Lightning, middle; and the Buck Hunter, bottom.

today. That's no exaggeration. The simple break-open action functions superbly as the basis of an in-line muzzleloader. Its barrel can easily be switched for a number of centerfire-rifle barrels or a 20-gauge barrel.

✓ The T/C Black Diamond is also a top-quality in-line rifle that borrows the best design features of all in-lines to date.

Traditions

The Traditions company offers a comprehensive line of reasonably priced Spanish-built muzzleloaders and accessories. Traditions

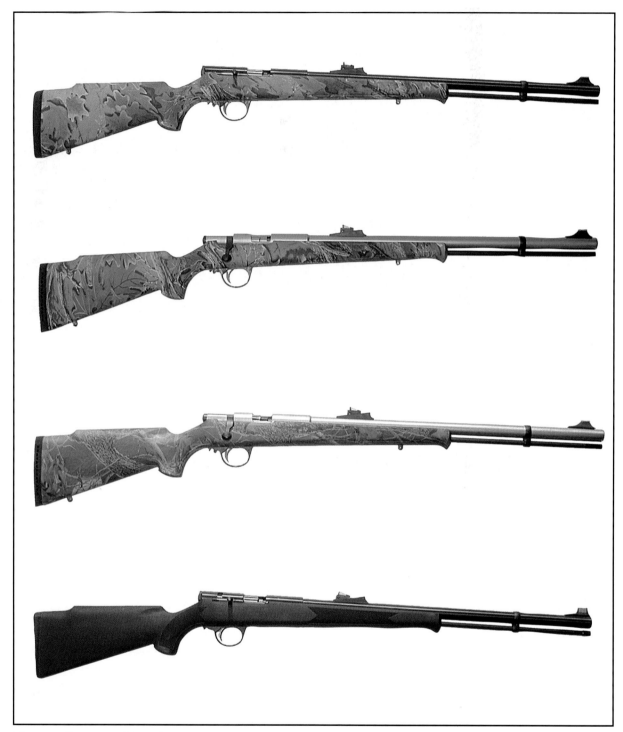

The CVA rifles pictured here, from top, are the Eclipse, Firebolt, Hunterbolt and Staghorn.

offers an amazing array of options throughout its product line.

✓ The Traditions Lightning is a miniature bolt-action in-line that cocks on the closing stroke. The Lightning looks and handles like a centerfire rifle, except for its ramrod.

✓ The Traditions Buckhunter is available in a variety of styles and options. This is a reliable, entry-level in-line rifle.

Both Traditions models are also sold by catalog retailers under different model names.

CVA

Connecticut Valley Arms, more popularly known as CVA, has been selling muzzleloaders

in North America for many years. CVA rifles are primarily entry-level models that are built in Spain.

✓ The CVA Apollo rifles were entry-level muzzleloaders that suffered a recall in the mid-1990s.

✓ The CVA Eclipse replaced the Apollo as an entry-level in-line. The Eclipse rifle is for those who can't spend a lot of money getting into muzzleloading.

✓ The CVA Stag Horn is a no-frills version of the Eclipse, and is a sound in-line rifle.

✓ The CVA Firebolt and Hunterbolt are smooth-handling bolt-action in-lines that offer many options and variations. The Hunterbolt is the basic version of this design.

Other In-Line Companies

✓ Millennium Designed Muzzleloaders is a relatively new company that is turning out nicely designed and built in-lines. The M2K rifle is one of the simplest, most accurate in-lines I have tested. This no-frills design makes for a reliable, well-built rifle. The MDM Buck-

waka is a low-priced, break-open in-line model. This in-line has clean, simple lines that enable left or right-hand shooting.

✓ The Kahnke Model 94 in-line design has been on the market several years and has proven to be a simple, reliable hunting rifle. The Kahnke bucks some trends by staying with blued steel and good walnut.

✓ Markesbery in-lines are Kahnke-style rifles complete with all of the bells and whistles such as stainless steel and composite stocks. The Markesbery offers the Black Bear, Brown Bear, Grizzly Bear and Polar Bear models.

✓ Remington modified its Model 700 center-fire bolt-action into an in-line muzzleloader that has the familiar look and feel of a Remington rifle. The 700ML is available in several configurations, including a youth model. The 700 ML features a composite

The short-lived Marlin MLS-50 is an in-line with an interchangeable cocking handle for left- or right-handed hunters, and an ambidextrous safety.

stock, bolt-action, removable breech plug and many other options unique to in-lines.

✓ Ruger also modified its tried-and-true M-77 short-cartridge action into an in-line muzzleloader. Ruger offers its in-line rifles in some interesting models, including the "Officer's Model," which has a straight grip and longer forend reminiscent of older frontier designs.

✓ Marlin's entry into the in-line field is a unique design that incorporates excellent features. The Marlin offers an interchangeable cocking handle for left- or right-hand use, as well as an ambidextrous safety on the tang.

✓ Austin and Halleck build in-lines that look more like custom centerfire rifles. They produce three models: the 420 in Monte Carlo and Classic, and the composite-stocked 320.

✓ Bass Pro Shops sells in-lines manufactured for them by Traditions. The rifles offer very good value.

✓ Cabela's also has in-line rifles made under their name. In the past, Cabela's also sold a "buffalo gun" look-alike based on the Remington rolling block. The Cabela's in-lines are a lot of rifle for the money.

✓ Dixie Gun Works markets an Italian Pedersoli rifle that it named the In-Line Carbine. Pedersoli also sells in-lines as the Gamma 9000, 900 and 901 models. These are traditional wood and steel rifles.

✓ The North American Arms Corp. manufactures the Gonic, a line of basic, well-made muzzleloaders. Gonic rifles have a unique .50-caliber barrel size, so only Gonic or specially dedicated bullets should be used in these rifles.

✓ Navy Arms markets an in-line called the Country Boy, which is imported from China. It's available at a reasonable price and offers good value.

✓ Lyman's in-line rifle was called the Cougar. This rifle suffered from continued production delays and did not get widely distributed.

Remington modified its popular Model 700 centerfire bolt-action to help make a popular in-line rifle.

✓ The Peifer Rifle Co. built a unique in-line rifle that featured excellent quality, an enclosed action and wonderful balance. The Peifer TS-93 was a hunter's rifle.

✓ Prairie River Arms built a line of in-lines. Its bull-pup design has the action directly under the shooter's face. Bullpup is a muzzleloader for someone who enjoys something "different." The Prairie River Arms is in a class by itself for ease of maintenance, and the little rifles perform well.

✓ White Shooting Systems built in-line rifles called the Super 91 and the Whitetail. These rifles had unique barrel diameters that necessitated the use of proprietary bullets only.

Conclusion

Obviously, this list could not include every possible in-line you'll stumble across, or that were manufactured after the year 2000. When looking at such lists and contemplating what is yet to come for in-line rifles, I can't help but marvel how quickly this branch of muzzleloading ignited interest in deer hunters. It went from a curiosity to the dominant force in muzzleloading in less than 10 years.

Back in 1985 when Tony Knight sold his first modern in-line, who would have believed that millions more of these rifles would soon be in use. Through it all, by the end of the 1900s, the in-line rifle ruled with muzzleloading deer hunters.

CHAPTER 4

Comparisons On and Off the Bench

After assembling a team of gun pros and hunters, the author had them analyze and rate today's muzzleloading rifles. Most of the rifles passed their stringent inspection. Keep these factors in mind when deciding which in-line to buy, but also realize that many decisions will be based mostly on available dollars and personal feel.

For several years I've been evaluating and making side-by-side comparisons of virtually all in-line rifles as they hit the market. Obviously, this work required me to develop a system to evaluate the rifles consistently. To do fair and comprehensive evaluations, I start my evaluation of each rifle by breaking it down on the gunsmith bench and analyzing the parts that make up the "machine." Next, I determine how well each rifle performs on the range. And third, I assess each rifle in the deer woods.

Compiling such a wide variety of data requires intense, objective scrutiny. This required me to get more shooters and hunters involved in the tests. Needless to say, I didn't have many problems getting the necessary assistance.

Tests and Record-Keeping

My primary test group was a five-man panel that carried out the detailed analysis of all major models on the gunsmith's bench. These men have an excellent variety of backgrounds, including careers as gunsmiths, professional machinists, computer technicians and other skills that contributed to our overall analysis of muzzleloaders. I also organized a group of experienced hunters who exclusively used various scoped in-lines for entire deer seasons so I could compile realistic information from the range and field. Simultaneously, I

The author developed a three-step system to analyze and rate today's various in-lines. Each rifle was inspected first on the gunsmith bench for workmanship and quality of parts. Next, it was tested at the range for feel and accuracy. Last, each rifle was tested for overall performance while hunting.

also supplied them with a variety of muzzle-loading bullets. After extensively testing these bullets on the range, we took them hunting and strived to recover them from big-game kills. Whenever we recovered them, we analyzed and recorded their performance.

The gunsmith's bench work involved examining the rifles using 17 criteria, which involved everything from "loseable" parts to quality of manufacture. We conducted these tests under uniform conditions, and maintained in-depth notes and records. All of our data sheets were computer-compatible. We started each test with a basic evaluation that recorded the rifle's caliber, weight, overall length, barrel length and twist rate, weight of trigger pull, number of safeties, type of steel and the type of breech plug. We also recorded the type of sights, stock, recoil pad, swivel studs, swivels, ramrod, and pertinent scope

base information.

During the bench analysis, we also recorded the number of parts in each rifle, and cataloged and described all plastic parts. The parts count included the stock, nipple, recoil pad, safety, springs, barreled action, breech plug, stock bolts, ramrod guides, trigger guard and screws, sling swivels and studs, bolt assembly, cocking handle, firing pin/hammer, end plug and pin or bolt, trigger assembly and bolts. We did not include ramrods or sight assemblies in the parts count.

When examining the various in-lines, we gathered at a facility that had several workbenches. Each evaluator had his own work space. By separating each inspector, we eliminated casual conversations that might influence opinions or create biases. Each man used the take-down tools that came with each rifle. We did not use any gunsmith tools that might have made the job easier. We rotated rifles to each station, trying to ensure each inspector was kept busy and did not have to wait long to examine each rifle. After a couple of sessions, the process became smooth and relatively efficient.

The author and his team of analysts rated eight handling factors for in-lines, including shouldering, balance, location of safety(s), operation of safety(s), trigger weight, trigger creep, trigger overtravel and overall weight. These are basic handling traits that prospective buyers should consider when choosing an in-line.

Analyzing Accessories

Besides evaluating the rifles ourselves, we also looked at the accessories, manuals and literature that accompanied each rifle. We started each evaluation by determining if the inspector was familiar with the particular rifle. Next, we had them read the instruction manual and rate how well it provided essential information for maintenance and use of the muzzleloader. Next, we suggested improvements that could be made to the manual. After that step, we examined the accessories that came with the muzzleloader, jotted down a starting time, and began disassembling the rifle as if for a basic cleaning. We then reassembled the rifle and noted the elapsed time, so we could compare the relative ease of basic disassembly and reassembly.

Then we stripped the rifle again and made a count of the total parts. During that count, we assessed the essential parts and parts that could be lost. By this point in the evaluation, the inspectors had examined the rifle thoroughly, and they gave their opinion about the quality of manufacturing and material selection. Then they rated the safety and trigger, and assessed the rifle's basic design. Next they assessed the gun's ease of maintenance, and finished the inspection by assessing the stock and sights, and the rifle's ambidexterity.

The Handling and Safety Tests

One of the most interesting tests we developed was called "blind handling." For this test, an inspector was blindfolded or went into a darkened room. He was then handed muzzleloaders one at a time. He handled the muzzleloader for 20 seconds, and then the record-keeper asked him to rate eight factors on a scale of 1 to 5.

After these evaluations, each inspector was handed a succession of in-lines to determine their personal favorite among the rifles. Each was given a rifle and allowed to handle it 15 seconds before getting another. Because we had so many rifles to test, we placed five in-

Accuracy was tested by two shooters using several test loads per model. Only the best group shot by each analyst was rated. A group smaller than 3 inches received an "A" rating, while a 3- to 6-inch group rated a "B," and a 6-inch-plus group rated a "C."

lines at a time on a table and narrowed them down to one favorite. Then we placed five more rifles on the table and repeated the process to select a favorite. When we had gone through the entire selection, we placed the favorites on the table, and each inspector assessed them to determine an overall winner.

The Rating Scale

As we conducted the tests, we used a set of criteria and ratings to determine relative scores. The rating scale we used was simple, with a range of 1 to 5 to quantify "poor" to "excellent."

The actual scale went as follows:

1: Definitely needs improvement; very poor fit, feel and accuracy

2: Not quite good enough; poor fit, feel and accuracy

3: Reasonable quality; average or normal fit, feel and accuracy

4: Well done; nice fit, feel and accuracy

5: Excellently done; exceptional fit, feel and accuracy

We rated eight handling factors on a scale of 1 to 5. Those factors were shouldering, balance, location of safety(s), operation of safety(s), trigger weight, trigger creep, trigger overtravel, and overall weight of each rifle.

These are basic handling traits that most prospective buyers should consider when choosing an in-line. The difference is that our testers usually didn't know which rifle they had in their hands. As a result, I found that the "blind-handling" tests provided some of the most practical information I've assembled for evaluating muzzleloaders.

Our inspectors used these rifles when hunting, which provided even more excellent information for the field/hunting assessments. Because we shot the rifles extensively on the range before the hunting season, our shooting evaluations included such items as relative ease of seating "dedicated" bullets, ease of capping or priming, and removing spent or unfired caps or primers. We also recorded the accuracy obtained with a standard test load and "custom" loads that each rifle shot best.

After all of those evaluations, we did a final test to determine how well the safeties func-

Bullet - Knight Red Hot 250 Gr.
Powder - Pyrodex Pellets 150 gr.
Speed - 2060 fps
Group - 1.3"

tioned. After removing each rifle's scopes and rings, and double-checking to ensure the rifles were unloaded, we put the safety on and smacked the rifle butt with a rubber hammer. None of the hammers dislodged as the safeties withstood the test. You might wonder why I didn't drop the rifles intentionally to replicate a fall in the field. I decided against that because all of the rifles weren't mine. I didn't want to be responsible for any damage.

The Shooting Test

After the bench tests, we took all of the rifles to the range to determine their accuracy potential. We only test-shot one rifle of each model in most cases. To indicate accuracy, we had a simple rating system. If the rifle shot a sub-3-inch group, we gave it an "A." A 3-inch to 6-inch group rated a "B," and a 6-inch-plus group rated a "C."

The test groups consisted of three shots at 100 yards fired by two shooters. To obtain each rating, we shot several test loads, and took the best groups. If each shooter had sub-2-inch groups with any load, we gave the rifle an "A." For the record, every rifle and load we tested would have hit within a deer's lethal zone at 100 yards, but some rifles were

The author tested virtually every in-line model on the market during recent years. All rifles tested were .50-caliber. They were fitted with detachable scope bases, allowing scopes to be used for all tests.

consistently more accurate than others.

The Test Rifles

Let's look at this pool of test candidates. I acquired new in-lines from virtually every company building these rifles. In addition, I also obtained several privately owned in-lines to beef up the test collection. To simplify the selection of components, I requested .50-caliber rifles. I then fitted most of the rifles with Weaver-style bases so we could use Leupold or Warne detachable rings, or standard Weaver rings, if necessary.

For the shooting tests we used the Nikon Monarch and Simmons Aetec riflescopes. These scopes are fine choices for in-line muzzleloaders. For the shooting tests, we set the scopes on their highest powers. I should note that we did not use the scopes during the handling trials, because we wanted to evaluate each rifle on its own merits. Our findings follow on the next four pages.

How Today's In-Line Muzzleloaders Rate

Modern Muzzleloading (Knight Rifles)

Knight MK-85

The MK-85 had the highest rating at 324 points. The MK-85 features two safeties, a removable breech plug, and many options. The MK-85 is the original modern in-line, but sadly, its days are numbered.
Grade: A

Knight LK-93

The Wolverine received 310 points. The LK-93 has the same basic features as the MK-85 except the barrel and action are integral. (The Wolverine is the first Knight in-line built with the barrel and receiver machined from one piece of steel. Previous models, such as early versions of the MK-85, have the barrel screwed into the receiver, similar to centerfire rifle design. The one-piece design is easier to manufacture and creates a stronger in-line. All Knight in-lines, including the MK-85, are now of integral barrel/receiver design, although the MK-85 has a machined lip to give it the look of a barrel screwed into the receiver.) The LK-93 received very uniform above-average marks except for the stock design.
Grade: A

Knight MK-95

The MK-95 received 312.5 points. This rifle uses a miniature bolt-action and special plastic .38 Special primer-holders for ignition. The basic design and stock-fit were slightly below the average of other items evaluated for this rifle.
Grade: A

Knight Big Horn

The Big Horn received 321 points. It earned evaluation marks very similar to the LK-93, except for the improved stock design.
Grade: A

Knight American Knight

The American Knight scored 319 points. This is the economy model of the LK-93. Its trigger is not adjustable and it is fitted with a cheaper stock. In all aspects of the tests, this rifle received above-average ratings.
Grade: A

Knight DISC Rifle

The DISC received 322 points, the highest rating of any bolt-action in-line on the market. The only concern about this rifle related to its lack of ambidexterity.
Grade: A

Knight T-Bolt

The T-Bolt received 290 points. This rifle had significantly more range in its ratings than any other Knight design. The inspectors' concerns were related to its design, maintenance and the stock fit.
Grade: A

Thompson/Center Arms

T/C Black Diamond
The Black Diamond scored 323 points, second highest in the test. This rifle obtained the most uniform scores in every aspect we tested. It received particularly high points for quality, design and handling. Even so, some individuals did not rate the stock design as high as other testers.
Grade: A

T/C 209X50
The Encore 209x50 scored 322 points. This break-open design in-line is extremely well-designed and solidly built. It received very high points for quality and maintenance, but lost a few points for its stock design and the trigger.
Grade: A

T/C System 1
The System 1 received 309 points. This is an oversized Firehawk at first appearance, but it has a removable barrel and breech-plug design. The System 1 received high marks, but some testers were concerned about its take-apart barrel design.
Grade: A

T/C Thunderhawk
The Thunderhawk received 302 points. This is a simple, robust in-line that offers solid performance. This rifle received uniformly high ratings except for its lack of an ambidextrous safety. The Thunderhawk does not use a removable breech plug.
Grade: A

T/C Firehawk
The Firehawk also received 302 points, which was interesting because it was scored during a different session than the almost-identical Thunderhawk. Again, uniformly high marks. The button safety was seen as an improvement, but is still not ambidextrous. No breech plug, but a great rifle.
Grade: A

T/C Scout
The Scout scored 260.5 points. The Scout is a carbine that's reminiscent of a Winchester Model 94, but without a lever. The Scout received strong marks for manufacturing quality, but it did not have a good trigger. It also lost points for handling and basic design.
Grade B

Traditions

Traditions' Buckhunter and Bass Pro Teflon Buckhunter
These rifles scored 254 and 255 points. They're simple, robust in-lines of basically sound design. Both rifles suffered significantly from below-average triggers and lack of ambidextrous safeties.
Grade: B

Traditions' Cabela's Timber Ridge
The Cabela's rifle scored 258. This reflects a better trigger and also simpler design. Although similar to the Buckhunter, the Timber Ridge design is simplified wherever possible.
Grade: B

Traditions Lightning
The Lightning scored 254.5. This bolt-action design is relatively simple. The rifle handled well but it suffered from a poor trigger and some rough machining.
Grade: B

Connecticut Valley Arms (CVA)

CVA Apollo
The Apollo received 257 points. We were surprised when this rifle was pulled from the market. Testers were concerned about its plastic parts and a poor trigger.
Grade: B

CVA Accubolt
The Accubolt received 265 points. This is a bolt-action design and is basically a sound in-line rifle. Its primary negative feature was a poor trigger.
Grade: A

Other Makes:

Austin and Halleck
The A&H in-line rifle received 300 points. This is a large bolt-action rifle that looks amazingly like a centerfire rifle. The A&H features excellent workmanship, a sound design and a very good trigger. The rifle is very large and quite heavy. As a result, it was downgraded for poor handling.
Grade: A

Cabela's Rolling Block
This Rolling Block scored 236 points. This Pedosoli built in-line is an impressive rifle. The rolling block is well-built, but suffers from a weight and balance problem compared to most in-lines tested.
Grade: B

Dixie Gun Works
This Pedosoli in-line scored 222 points. This somewhat heavy and "over-designed" rifle is still a decent in-line. Balance, trigger and weight received below-average ratings.
Grade: B

Gonic GA-93
The GA-93 scored 287 points. Gonic rifles are notable for nice workmanship and simple design. Gonic in-lines employ a unique bore diameter that limits the choice of projectiles. The rifle was judged to be heavy, which effected its handling qualities.
Grade: A

Kahnke M-94
The M-94 scored 235 points. This is a unique design that is somewhat similar to the T/C Scout. The Kahnke is one of the simplest and most robust in-line designs conceived. The trigger on this rifle scored lower than most aspects evaluated.
Grade: B

Markesbery Black Bear
The Black Bear scored 232 points. This is a Kahnke design, so anything said about the M-94 applies to the Markesbery. The Markesbery line has many options that change the handling and appearance of the basic rifle.
Grade: B

Marlin MLS-50

The Marlin scored 300.5 points. This is a great-handling little rifle that resembles the T/C Firehawk. The Marlin received good marks for its trigger, handling and overall quality. It received below-average marks for ease of maintenance. The Marlin was judged the most ambidextrous in-line on the market, with its tang safety and "switchable" cocking handle.

Grade: A

Millennium Designed Muzzleloader: M2K

The M2K scored 315 points. This is a simple, robust in-line with good design, manufacture, excellent trigger and easy maintenance. The rifle has a blocky stock design that slightly hampered its handling.

Grade: A

Navy Arms Country Boy

The Country Boy scored 223 points. This is a good entry-level in-line. It has a very simple, robust design that is fairly well machined. It suffers from a poor trigger and did not balance well when its accessories were stored inside the stock.

Grade: B

Peifer TS-93

The TS-93 received 314 points. This fine in-line has been discontinued, which is a shame. The Peifer is a unique design featuring a sealed action, removable priming devices, and a cocking lever incorporated into the trigger guard. Ease of maintenance was the only consideration for this rifle.

Grade: A

Prairie River Arms Bull-pup

The PRA bull-pup scored 230 points. This is the most unique in-line we evaluated. The bull-pup design goes against most ideas of what a muzzleloader should look like, but we found it to be a good-shooting rifle. It received good marks for quality, but did not fare well with design and handling criteria.

Grade: B

Remington M700 ML

The M700 ML scored 288 points. This is an impressive bolt-action style rifle. This rifle received above-average points for quality and it had an excellent trigger. The 700ML lost points for balance and weight.

Grade: A

Ruger Model 77-50

The 77-50 scored 305.5 points. This little Ruger is a bolt-action carbine style in-line that handles beautifully. The Ruger received above-average points for quality, balance and weight. The ease of maintenance was the only below-average consideration.

Grade: A

White S-91

The Super 91 was scored 299.5 points. This is a well made in-line that features a reliable, simple design. The S-91 also has an odd-ball bore dimension that necessitates "fouling" the bore before seating a bullet. This rifle has not been built for a long time, but efforts to resurrect it occasionally go on.

Grade: A

The author found a common occurrence among most bolt-action in-lines — gumming. Because bolt-actions have tighter tolerances and more moving parts, powder residue from repeated shots often made the bolt actions stick and difficult to operate. Therefore, bolt-actions require more care and cleaning to keep them functioning reliably.

Getting What You Pay for

An amazing number of in-line muzzleloaders entered the market during the last 15 years of the 1900s. I was impressed with the consistent quality available in these rifles. The standard line, "you get what you pay for," applies to in-line rifles, which the evaluation charts and graphs affirm.

One of the most obvious differences in the rifles is trigger quality, especially between offshore and American-made in-lines, but virtually all in-line triggers can be adjusted. Another difference was in barrel quality, with U.S.-made barrels generally featuring smoother finishes and more uniform bore dimensions. The American-made rifles also typically had better finishes, with better polishing and fewer tool marks, but these factors don't affect whether a buck hits the ground or not.

Interestingly, after working on this in-line inspection project, some of the panel members still couldn't decide which one to buy for themselves. I sense that dollars and personal feel will be the major factors in deciding which in-line to buy.

The Test Results

After countless hours of shooting and analyzing data, what did we find? This might sound like a cop-out, but the data revealed that most of the in-lines we tested are surprisingly close to each other in quality, handling and performance. Some of them clearly earned higher scores, and some had scores indicating serious problems. With the high-quality materials and modern technology used to make parts, all of these guns should be well made, but this is not always the case. The biggest differences we found were in design, not manufacturing.

Fouling and Gumming

If you're most interested in the in-line's shooting performance reviews, that's coming up. We shot the rifles extensively on the range and during hunts. I'll review our "out-of-the-box" accuracy tests in Chapter 7.

These extensive tests revealed an interesting side note: some in-lines do not handle residue. Invariably, the more complex in-line designs started having problems after a small amount of shooting.

The primary culprits are bolt-action in-lines, because of their close tolerances and many parts. They "bung-up" with heavy use. We had various problems with every bolt-action design we tested, ranging from failure to fire after as few as seven shots, to corroding so tightly shut that we could not open the bolt. The problem is so widespread that it does no good to single out any one bolt-action. They all require more care and cleaning than simpler designs to ensure they function reliably. As the manufacturers stress, stripping and cleaning the inside of the bolt is the most important consideration when cleaning and maintaining these in-lines.

Keep in mind, however, that our shooting tests involved much more shooting than anyone would do during a day of deer hunting. However, by doing such intensive shooting, we reconfirmed what we already knew: a poorly maintained in-line will invariably fail when the buck of a lifetime steps out. Whenever you shoot these in-lines, clean them. And when you clean a bolt-action, break down the bolt and thoroughly clean it.

At the other end of the spectrum, we shot a Knight Wolverine in-line rifle 125 consecutive shots one day, with only minor cleaning of "grunge" from the action area. We also shot a T/C Thunderhawk 125 straight shots and this rifle performed just as well late in the day as it did when we began shooting. Try that with any bolt-action on the market!

I realize no one shoots 100-plus shots in a day of hunting, but it proves that some in-lines are inherently more reliable and require less service than others to keep functioning. The bolt-action just isn't designed to handle black-powder marathon shooting tests. Some bolt-actions are modified from centerfire designs, which were never engineered to contend with corrosive residue in the quantities created by black powder or its substitutes.

Therefore, when you're on the range and focusing on accuracy, be equally aware of how well your rifle will operate as it becomes fouled. If this factor isn't always on your mind, you'll one day be reminded when it's too late.

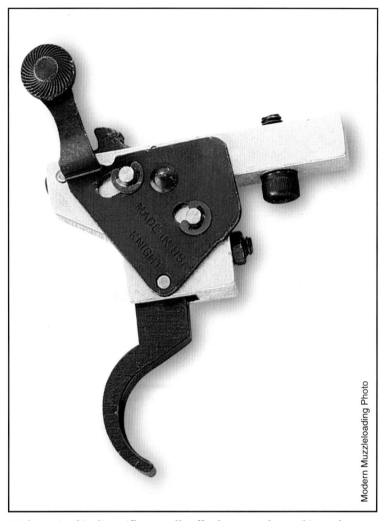

Higher-priced in-line rifles usually offer better workmanship and components. In addition, the author found that triggers and barrel quality were held to higher standards when made by U.S. companies.

These rifles have also been responsible for many hunters entering the sport. Invariably, a friend who accompanies us on a hunt decides to buy an in-line rifle. Why? Because it's fun and challenging. Another side benefit has resulted from these new in-line hunters: My bullet collection continues increasing after each hunting season.

Conclusion

The test group of in-lines discussed in this chapter have accounted for a significant number of deer, and they were continuing to do so as the 2000 deer season approached.

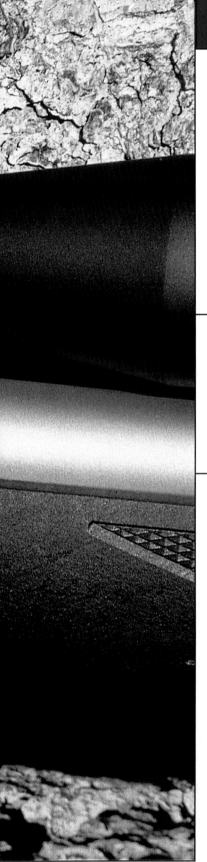

CHAPTER 5

Fire and Smoke: Part 1, Fire

No matter which of the three ignition devices lights the charge, muzzleloading velocities remain fairly constant. The primary advantage of musket caps and 209 shotshell primers over No. 11 percussion caps is their ease of handling. All three "primers" produce enough fire to ignite Pyrodex or black powder.

Flint or percussion? Those were the choices in muzzle-loading rifles for a couple of centuries in North America. Shooters also had two choices for projectiles: conical slugs or patched round-balls. And there was only one propellant: black powder.

Beginning in 1985, however, the in-line muzzleloading craze has caused more advancements for black-powder hunters than occurred during the previous 200 years. Today's muzzleloading hunters can choose from a bewildering array of bullet styles, weights and diameters; not to mention color-coded sabots. They also have more choices in propellants and cleaners, which allow what old timers could only dream about: no messy, foul-smelling cleaning sessions with boiling water and barrels of elbow grease!

Besides improved propellants and sophisticated saboted bullets, manufacturers are constantly improving ignition systems with hotter, longer-lasting flame temperatures. These ignition systems enhance the performance of recently invented propellants such as the Hodgdon Pyrodex Pellet. Although technology has made significant advances over the slow, "flash-boom" associated with flintlock ignitions, the possibility of misfires or hang-fires still exists. These problems can occur when little or no spark or flame reaches the powder charge. Contaminated powder charges and blocked flame paths — resulting from debris in the nipple

Before 1985, muzzleloading whitetail hunters had few options. Black powder was the only propellant, flint or percussion caps were the only ignition devices, and conical slugs and patched round-balls were the only projectiles available.

and/or breech plug — can also cause problems in the most modern of muzzleloaders.

The Flame Channel

The basic design of sidehammer muzzleloaders requires that fire from the ignited percussion cap angles down into the chamber, or combustion area. It all starts with the cap, which is perched on a nipple. When the falling hammer crushes the cap against the nipple, fire spurts from the cap and is channeled down through the hole in the nipple's center. The flame bursts out of the nipple and into the powder chamber, where it ignites the black-powder charge. This causes a controlled detonation or explosion, driving the projectile down the barrel and toward the deer.

This simple design has a few inherent flaws, however. The nipple is mounted on the top side of the barrel, exposing it to the elements. The nipple's location also increases the chance

that the cap could fall off or be knocked off. Enter the in-line design, whose concept dates back a few centuries, even though it was never accepted as widely as the caplock.

Not until Tony Knight developed a simple, reliable, straight-line action did the in-line muzzleloading rifle start attracting attention. Knight threaded a breech plug into one end of the barrel to contain the powder charge. Before installing the plug, Knight drilled and threaded a small hole through its center so a nipple could be threaded on directly behind the powder charge. When the cap was detonated, the fire burst directly into the combustion chamber. The distance between cap and charge was short and direct, unlike the longer, twisting path inherent to sidelocks.

Priming a muzzleloader is a crucial element in preparing for a shot. The easier this task, the better, especially during those intense moments when a quick second shot is required.

Why Ignition Differences Matter

Some ignition systems are more user-friendly than others. Some muzzleloaders I've used have ignition systems that are extremely annoying. Their key components did not fit together

In-line shooters can choose from three ignition devices: the musket cap, left; shotshell primer, center; and the No.11 percussion cap. Musket caps deliver about three times the flame of percussion caps, and shotshell primers deliver about four times the flame of percussion caps.

properly. More than one buck got a new lease on life because a cap fell off the nipple or the ignition flame died in a too-easily fouled ignition channel.

I'll never forget the morning I watched a tremendous white-tailed buck flag his way across a wide valley after a close brush with doom. I had rattled the buck into range of my son, Glen, who was less than 100 yards from the buck's nose when he squeezed the trigger. All three of us — Glen, I and the buck — heard the dull metallic click. The huge whitetail spun and ran away, a bit scared but no less healthy than he had been at dawn that day. Glen hadn't noticed that the percussion cap had slipped off his in-line's nipple.

I had a similar experience during a recent hunt with Knight for desert mule deer in New Mexico. Vegetation obscured the front of a wide-antlered buck, so I got up and sneaked 15 yards to a better site. The buck was now standing broadside at 75 yards. A beautiful sunrise sky accentuated his size and appearance. I'll never forget the sight. Nor will I forget the sound of the hammer falling on my rifle's suddenly empty nipple. The oversized musket cap had obviously fallen off when I moved. The

muley didn't give me a second chance. It quickly disappeared into heavier cover.

Access to the Ignition System

I evaluate many in-line rifles each year, and I always check the access to the nipple or ignition area. Many actions do not have an adequate opening for placing a cap onto the nipple with your fingers. This makes me assume that rifle designers believe everyone has a capper. Or that hunters have tiny fingers. I've shot several in-line rifles that I could not cap with my big, clumsy fingers. On the other hand, some designs make the job easy by ensuring the action is cut adequately to expose the nipple.

In-line shooters can usually choose from three ignition devices: the traditional No. 11 percussion cap, the larger musket cap, or modern shotgun or rifle primers. The flame volume varies, with musket caps delivering

Because the basic nipple hole and thread dimensions are identical on many in-line muzzleloading rifles, nipples for percussion caps and musket caps can be interchanged easily.

roughly three times the flame of percussion caps, and No. 209 shotgun primers quadrupling the output of percussion caps. In addition, shotgun primers produce gases 700 degrees hotter than those produced by No. 11 percussion caps.

Each ignition system has advantages and disadvantages to consider. Some rifles, in fact, can be set up to shoot all three ignition devices. Because the basic nipple hole and thread dimensions are identical, nipples for percussion caps and musket caps can be interchanged easily.

No. 11 Percussion Caps

First, let's look at the No. 11 percussion cap, which is one of the oldest and most widely used ignition sources for muzzleloaders. The bottom of a percussion cap holds an impact-sensitive explosive mixture. When the hammer strikes the cap, it sets off a significant flame.

RWS, CCI and Remington make No. 11 percussion caps that fit virtually any muzzleloader, be it an in-line or a sidehammer. Percussion caps are the smallest of the three ignition devices, so they're slightly more awkward to handle. However, many excellent cappers are available. Cappers store a supply of caps and help the shooter place a cap on the nipple.

No. 11 percussion caps have been the standard for many years, and continue to excel at igniting black powder. About the only recent development in this cap was CCI's introduction of the No. 11 Magnum percussion cap, which is noticeably hotter and offers improved performance.

When "snapping caps" before loading the powder charge, the report from CCI's No. 11 Magnum caps is noticeably louder than the sound of standard caps. Although I cannot determine any velocity difference when chronographing shots ignited by both varieties of No. 11 caps, I'm confident the extra spark created by magnum caps ensures more uniform ignition. This is particularly significant in cold weather, because I never have any hangfires or delayed ignition problems when using the magnum No. 11s.

Musket Caps

Musket caps have also been around a long time, and are often called "top-hats" because of the prominent rim around their base. These caps are significantly larger than No. 11 percussion caps and generate significantly more flame, but they're technically a percussion cap. CCI and RWS manufacture musket caps. RWS caps come with four or six flanges — or slits — in the rim. I cannot detect a performance difference between the two versions. With the sudden popularity of musket-cap ignition systems in the late 1990s, manufacturers rushed to design oversized cappers to handle its unique flange shape. Musket caps, however, are large enough to easily seat on most nipples using your fingers.

Rifle and Shotgun Primers

By the mid-1990s, manufacturers were looking for even hotter ignition sources. Rifle and shotgun primers were incorporated into muzzleloader ignition systems because of their hotter, longer flames. These primers require a special holder or a chamber-style recess in the rifle's action. Rifle primers — usually of the small-rifle magnum type — required special

Although percussion caps and musket caps are widely used, many "high-performance" in-lines use No. 209 shotshell primers. Some in-lines were engineered to use handgun and small-rifle primers, but they never became as popular as in-lines using shotshell primers. Shown above is the plastic disc and 209 primer used in the popular Knight DISC Rifle.

holders, including plastic .38 Special cartridge cases used in the Knight Magnum Elite rifle. Knight and Markesbery marketed small rifle-primer ignitions for a while, but interest in these products never took off. Several aftermarket companies offered rifle-primer holders that fit over the nipple. These never achieved popularity, because they proved slow to work with.

The No. 209 shotgun primer ignition systems quickly became popular and are found on most "high-performance" in-lines. Shotgun primers are placed directly into a chamber in the breech plug of the T/C Encore 209x50. Shotgun primers can also be inserted into bright orange plastic holders used in Knight's DISC rifle. Shotgun primers are the most weather-resistant ignition device, and they're also large enough to easily handle.

Ignition Velocity Test

Ignition Style	Summer (72 degrees F)	Winter (-15 degrees F)
No. 11 Percussion Cap	1,594 fps	1,544 fps
Musket Cap	1,587 fps	1,536 fps
209 Shotshell Primer	1,610 fps	1,567 fps

Figure 5-1. Do the various ignition devices produce different velocities? To find out, the author chronographed shots from a variety of rifles using 100 grains of Pyrodex RS powder and a saboted 300-grain bullet. The rifles also had similar barrel lengths. In addition, he conducted the tests in summer and winter to see if temperature was a contributing factor.

Are There Real Advantages?

What are the actual advantages of these "newer" ignition styles? Not much really, because the volume of flame that reaches the propellant is governed by the size of the nipple hole, breech-plug hole, and the length of the ignition path. Breech plugs that are unnecessarily long also reduce flame temperatures. All three ignition devices produce temperatures several times hotter than required to ignite Pyrodex and black powder.

Although most percussion- and musket-cap breeches are too small for easy access with fingers, the 209-primed rifles are easy to work with. I particularly like the break-open 209x50 from T/C. This remarkable in-line is the easiest muzzleloader to prime. The 209x50 and the Peifer are unique in having sealed actions. This results in better performance, and eliminates dirty scope bodies and debris throughout the action area.

The plastic holders used in Knight DISC rifles to position No. 209 shotgun primers fit nicely into the forward portion of the bolt. Because of these holders, DISC rifles are easy to prime and unprime, as long as the bolt cutout is free of debris.

Do these three ignition devices produce different velocities? I wanted to know this, so I chronographed shots from a variety of rifles using similar barrel lengths and loads (see Figure 5-1). The Knight DISC rifle offers the opportunity to use No. 11 percussion caps or No. 209 shotgun primers, while the T/C Black Diamond can be set up for No. 11 or musket caps. Because the velocities I obtained during summer shooting did not indicate any clear advantage between the ignition devices, I repeated the tests during extremely cold weather. The accompanying chart shows velocities obtained during summer (+72 degrees Fahrenheit) and winter shooting (-15 degrees Fahrenheit) with the same rifles and loads. As you can see, there was little difference between the test results, despite different ignition systems and an 87-degree difference in air temperature.

Mock Field Tests

Besides checking velocities, I also tested the caps and primers for field-handling characteristics. Using CCI musket caps and CCI No. 11 caps, I placed a cap on its appropriate nipple and removed it, replaced it and removed it for 10 cycles. I did this five times with each style of cap. The No. 11 caps became a little looser in fit, but they all fired at the end of each test. The musket caps also loosened up, and one of the caps lost all of its ignition chemical after seven recaps. The other four musket caps fired, but they became noticeably looser in fit than the No. 11 caps.

I also loaded and unloaded 10 shotshell primers into a T/C 209x50 exactly 20 times each and they all fired. Granted, mine wasn't a scientific test, nor does it statistically indicate any repeatable trends, but it shows it's possible for caps to lose their vital ignition chemicals if repeatedly placed on the nipple. No matter if the cap has been used once or 10 times, always check to ensure the ignition chemicals haven't been dislodged.

After doing the cap/uncap tests, I dropped each type of cap and primer into a bowl of water. I removed each quickly after the immersion, and blew them clear of water, much as a hunter would do if this occurred afield. I put 10 of each type through this water test, and

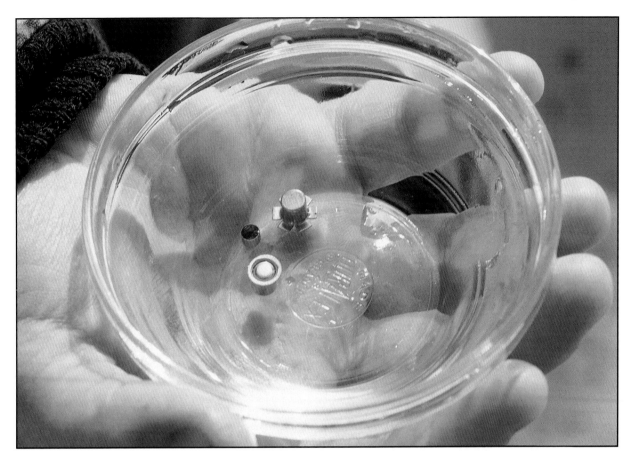

they all fired. Then I soaked 10 of each type in water for one minute. Again, everything fired. Finally I soaked 10 more for five minutes, stirring them to ensure there no air bubbles were keeping moisture from the chemical. All of the 209s fired, all of the musket caps fired, but only four No. 11s fired.

I used a T/C Black Mountain magnum side-hammer for the musket caps and No. 11 percussion caps, switching nipples for each style. This subjected each cap to the same hammer strike. I used a Knight DISC rifle for the 209 primers.

Which is Best?

Although velocities remain fairly constant, the primary advantage of musket caps and 209 shotshell primers over No. 11 percussion caps is their ease of handling. To allow shooters to pick their own preferred system, some manufacturers offer all three systems in one package. This is a great idea, because owners can then experiment and use the ignition type of their choice. Until a clear favorite establishes itself in the market, I expect most manufacturers will try to offer similar ignition packages.

Which is best? I'd say it's probably the

The author conducted mock field tests with each ignition device to determine durability and reliability. He placed 10 of each ignition device in a bowl of water, quickly removed them, blew them clear of water, and fired each. He then repeated the test, soaking 10 more of each device for one minute, and 10 more for five minutes. On the long test, only four of the No. 11 percussion caps fired.

modern 209 shotgun primer systems. Why? They have the best ignition capabilities, plus they're extremely water-resistant and the most easy to handle.

On a different issue, should this modern technology be incorporated into black-powder firearms? Why not? Stainless steel and plastic composites have virtually replaced blued steel and walnut. Muzzleloader hunters want user-friendly firearms, and the new ignition systems satisfy that demand.

The "17 Misfires Buck"

When it comes to ignition problems, however, I probably hold some kind of record for the most frustrating hunting experience in recent times. The location was a ranch in western Texas. The muzzleloader was a prototype, and it had shot superbly on the range before

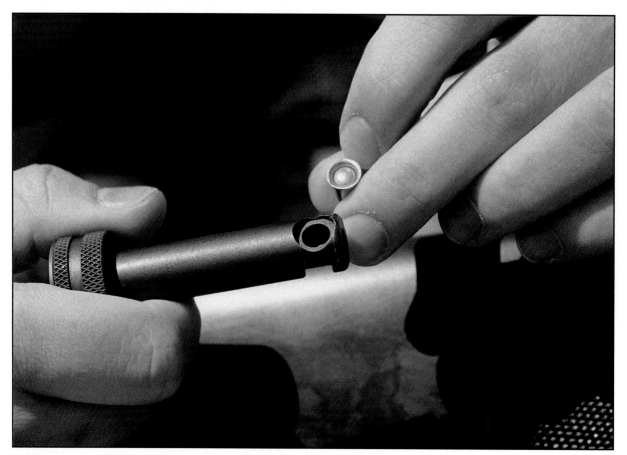

The author says the No. 209 shotgun primer is the best ignition device based on water-resistance, ease of handling and ignition capabilities. The primer holder above fits the discontinued Peifer TS-93 rifle.

the hunt. The caps, also new, were early-production items, but they seemed OK. The propellant? It was fresh and state-of-the-art.

On the last morning of our hunt we spotted a respectable 5-by-5 white-tailed buck courting a nearly ready doe. He was not about to leave her side. Everything was perfect. Early-morning light illuminated the buck's coat and made for a wonderful picture. I waited patiently for the perfect opportunity. At about 60 yards, the buck stepped clear of some cactus and I put the cross-hairs on its chest. There was no need to rush. I took my time aiming. After controlling my breathing, I released a half-breath, and slowly put pressure on the trigger. Everything was perfect. This was a guaranteed deal. The buck looked back at the doe, and the hammer fell.

"Snap!" No boom! I quickly removed the fired cap from the nipple and put on another. The buck hadn't moved an inch. I repeated the first sequence: breathing, sight picture, trigger

control and cross-hairs on the chest. All of this went through my mind as I wondered why the muzzleloader had not fired.

"Snap!" Again no boom! Was it the caps? The propellant? Did I "dry-ball" that morning, forgetting to put in powder before sliding the bullet home? Was the nipple blocked? The buck moved a few steps and looked over his shoulder toward me. He was still far more concerned about his doe than me, and maybe for good reason!

Again I went through the firing ritual, and again heard a disheartening pop. The sound did not disturb the love-struck buck, and I tried several more times with no success.

Finally, my patient guide suggested we sneak away and clean the rifle. We slowly left the scene and slipped behind a big hill downwind from the deer. I quickly removed the nipple and checked to ensure it was clear. Then we frantically pulled the bullet and were rewarded with a handful of dry propellant. I ran a dry patch through the bore, reinstalled the nipple and carefully reloaded. Just to be sure, I fired a shot into the dirt. Then we quickly went through the reloading procedure and quietly returned to the same location. The buck was

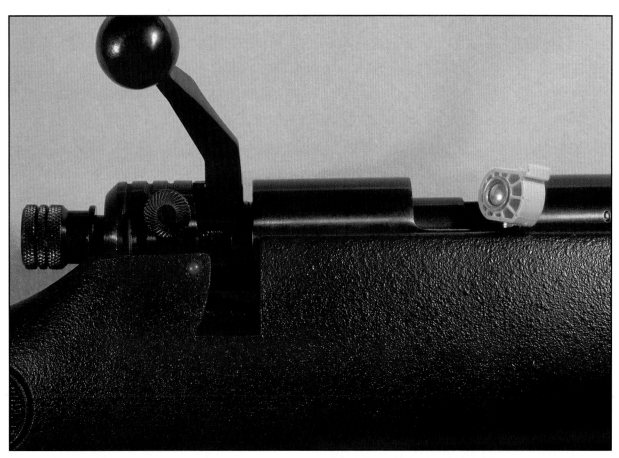

still tending, only a few yards from where we had left him!

Once again I set up for a shot: good rest, no rush, take your time — do it right. But with a familiar "pop," the ignition again failed. And again. And again. Five more tries. With our tails between our legs, we retreated again behind the hill and repeated the take-down performance.

Back again, same buck, same scenario. Love is a powerful thing. That old buck was still in the same place near the hot, bedded doe in the scrub brush. This time he was a little spooky, looking at us more than before, but after a few minutes he stood broadside again. The guide "lasered" him at 75 yards, and I went through the familiar drill.

"Snap!" Again and again. Each time I went through the whole shooting sequence just in case the rifle fired. After five more failures, we looked at each other, grinned and decided the buck deserved to live. Then again, we didn't seem to be in any position to make him otherwise! I had snapped a total of 17 caps on that buck, and I was really tired of the situation.

I had touched off each shot perfectly, just in case the rifle actually fired! I still had to

Should modern technology, such as shotgun primers, be incorporated into black-powder firearms? The author believes so. In-line hunters want user-friendly firearms, and the new ignition systems satisfy that demand. Shown above is the Knight DISC rifle. The orange device holds the primer in place, eliminating the need for a nipple.

concentrate to ensure a good hit. But 17 misfires is as many as I want to shoot at any critter.

To this day, I still don't know the exact cause of the misfires. Talking to many experts only makes the story sillier. Everyone has their opinions, but no one can really say what went wrong.

Maybe that buck was just standing atop a bag of horseshoes.

CHAPTER 6

Fire and Smoke: Part 2, Smoke

Actual black powder is declining rapidly in use. Like the long rifles of old, black powder is succumbing to modern substitutes and the realities of its own inherently dangerous properties. Nothing is pushing black powder faster toward the brink than the Pyrodex Pellet. This phenomenon is driven by the pellet's convenience, consistency and reliability.

Some muzzleloading advice seems timeless. For example, there's this old standby: "Throw in about a hundred grains of powder and she'll shoot OK." Or how about this one: "Start at 80 grains and work up to a hundred or 110."

Those words, or similar ones, hold true whether you're discussing flintlocks, sidelocks or the latest in-lines. Most muzzleloading rifles will show a preference for a charge of 80 to 100 grains, simple as that. Of course, several in-lines are designed to handle and perform with significantly heavier charges, with 150 grains being the norm.

Although the term "black powder" is almost a generic description of muzzleloading propellants, most of us realize the real black powder differs from its modern equivalents, such as Pyrodex. Actual black powder, however, is declining rapidly in use. Like the long rifles of old, black powder is succumbing to modern substitutes and the realities of its own inherently dangerous properties. In fact, the days of black powder as a hunting propellant are probably numbered. Why? Because there are just too many reasons for it to die out.

Why Black Powder is Flaming Out

Without getting technical, black powder is dangerous, and it has some nasty habits when used in firearms. First, it's an explosive.

The term "black powder" is often used as a generic description of muzzleloading propellants. Actual black powder use, however, is declining as black powder substitutes, such as Pyrodex, gain favor.

Instead of burning in a progressive, controllable rate, it detonates. When a spark hits it, an explosion instantly results, causing energy to rapidly release. After the boom, noxious residues remain to attract moisture. Chemical changes then occur, which encourage rust to quickly form.

In addition, many governmental branches at the city and national level, are uncomfortable with black powder. Increasingly stringent regulations make black powder more difficult to market. Many jurisdictions do not allow it to be stored and sold in large malls, which eliminates the product from many sporting-goods chains. Just how long black powder remains available for public use is a matter of question.

The picture is not bleak, however, because companies such as Hodgdon offer products that emulate the power and performance of black powder, but without its inherent storage, transportation and public-safety concerns.

With so many hunters shooting muzzleload-ers, propellants are a major factor in the sport's viability. Manufacturers continue the quest to make in-lines more user-friendly, and this includes improving the propellants. Although the new propellants feature significantly better "hydroscopic" properties, rust is still a concern.

Black Powder's Virtues, Challenges

Black powder is still a great propellant and will continue to have loyal users for many years, despite its bleak long-term future. Many shooters believe they obtain their best accuracy with black powder. The biggest concern is that black powder requires immediate cleaning after shooting to prevent rust from forming.

When you shoot a muzzleloader, two things happen. First, the shot scrapes away material, exposing spots of bare, unprotected steel inside the bore. Meanwhile, the shot leaves behind residues. These residues can be compared to tiny sponges, which will grab and hold water. Quite simply, laying wet sponges atop bare metal quickly results in rust.

How can the shooter prevent rust from forming? The answer is simple: Run some moisture-displacing oil down the bore after shooting, and also break the breech plug free and clean it. The "sponges" will fill up with the oil, making things difficult for rust. Even if you don't immediately remove the residue, it becomes relatively inert and prevents rust from forming. Of course, this is just a temporary solution. You should give the rifle a good cleaning as soon as possible.

Tony Knight adamantly believes that ruined muzzleloader barrels are never shot-out. Virtually all such barrels are destroyed by poor cleaning and preservation. In other words, neglect. He is no doubt correct, particularly with in-lines. Why? With in-lines, no lube is required for loading bullets enclosed by a soft-plastic sabot. As a result, the sabot applies no protective coating to the barrel. In addition, the sabot lightly "scrubs" the metal during loading and firing, exposing the bore to powder residues.

Black Powder Specifics

Two major suppliers produce black powder in North America: Goex and Buffalo. Black powder is differentiated by granule

Black powder is an excellent propellant, and many shooters believe they obtain their best accuracy with it. However, black powder leaves behind caustic, water-attracting residue after firing. Immediate cleaning is required to prevent rust from forming inside the barrel.

size. During the manufacturing process, the powder is screened through various sieves, thereby separating it by granule size. The coarseness of black powder is indicated by a designation system using the letter "F" followed by the letter "G." The more F's, the less coarse the powder. Therefore, FFFG is a finer grade powder than FFG. Its kernels, or granules, are smaller and burn more quickly.

FFG and FFFG perform similarly, providing excellent accuracy and uniform ignition with in-lines. FFFG appears to burn more cleanly in most rifles, with noticeably less residue on cleaning patches. I find that black powder provides extremely uniform performance. Virtually every rifle shoots accurately with

loads ranging from 80 to 100 grains. Black powder also meters nicely through powder flasks, particularly the finer FFFG.

Pyrodex Powders

Hodgdon offers four Pyrodex products. The basic Pyrodex RS is equivalent to FFG black powder, although possibly not quite as easy to ignite. Pyrodex P, for pistol, works beautifully as a rifle powder. And because it's of signifi-

The coarseness of black powder is indicated by a designation system using the letter "F" followed by the letter "G." The more F's, the finer the powder.

Hodgdon's Pyrodex is offered in grades similar to black powder. Coarseness affects the powder's burning characteristics and, in turn, pressure.

100 Grains by Volume: Actual Weight of Powder

Powder Type	Weight
Goex FFG	101.3
Goex FFFG	101.6
Goex Clear Shot	95.1
Pyrodex Select	63.9
Pyrodex RS	72.5
Pyrodex P	73.0
Pyrodex Pellets	74.2
Arco	94.7
Clean Shot	85.1
Quick Shots	65.3

Figure 6-1. To show that some powders are bulkier than others, the author compared the volume of various propellants to their weight.

cantly finer granulation, it appears to leave less residue than RS or Pyrodex Select.

Pyrodex Select is the bulkiest Pyrodex, with uniformly large granules that yield slightly less pressure than P and RS. Select is very consistent and generally shoots well in all muzzleloaders. Pyrodex Select, however, is a little too bulky to meter smoothly through most powder flasks. An occasional tap on the flask is needed to keep it flowing.

The fourth Pyrodex product is the most exciting propellant available to in-line hunters. Pyrodex Pellets, formed by compressing Pyrodex RS into 45-caliber cylinders, are easy to use. Pellets provide the most uniform ignition and burning characteristics of any propellant I've tested. The little 30- and 50-grain cylinders eliminate concerns about compaction, moisture content and weight uniformity. In chronographing more than 175 different tests in a wide variety of muzzleloaders, Pyrodex Pellets have provided the most consistent shot-to-shot performance.

Clear Shot Powder

Clear Shot is a black-powder substitute from Goex that took years to develop. Clear Shot resembles coarse ball-powder. Its spheres are dark gray to black and vary in size and shape. Clear Shot pours easily through flasks and measurers, which makes for uniform charges for shooting. My tests indicate slightly lower velocities with Clear Shot, but it produces accurate shots and crisp ignition. Hopefully the growing pains are over and Clear Shot will become available to muzzleloader hunters.

Other Powders

Other black-powder substitutes are also available, but not as readily as the powders mentioned earlier. Perhaps that will change with time.

Arco Black Mag was available for a time in the United States. Although expensive, the powder was well received. For unknown reasons, however, it disappeared from the shelves. This bulky, grayish white powder does not contain sulfur, so the age-old concern about rusting is eliminated.

Arco has a slightly lower yield than other powders, so loads have to be adjusted upward 10 percent or 15 percent to obtain similar

Velocity Test: Black Powder and Black-Powder Substitutes

Powder Type (100 grains)	Velocity (feet per second)
Goex FFG	1,468
Goex FFFG	1,553
GOEX CLEAR SHOT	1,404
Pyrodex SELECT	1,523
Pyrodex RS	1,580
Pyrodex P	1,594
Pyrodex PELLETS	1,570
ARCO	1,384
CLEAN SHOT	1,366
QUICK SHOTS	1,233

Figure 6-2. The author tested various 100-grain powder charges by shooting a 300-grain hollow-point bullet through a chronograph placed 10 feet from the muzzle.

performance. Arco is also bulky, and does not meter smoothly through most powder flasks. I pour it straight from the can, and use a small funnel to direct it into the powder measure.

Clean Shot Powder is made by Clean Shot Technologies Inc., and has been relatively accessible throughout the United States. Clean Shot resembles Arco Black Mag in appearance, but it contains no sulfur, so it's much less corrosive. I have found Clean Shot to be clean-burning, but the bullet speeds it produces are usually slightly less than those obtained with black powder or Pyrodex. I've also found that velocities and accuracy improved when I made a point of very firmly seating the projectiles.

Quick Shots are essentially 100-grain equivalent compressed pellets of Clean Shot powder. These pellets offer the cleaner-burning properties of Clean Shot, and are intended for .50-caliber rifles. I tested an early production lot of Quick Shot pellets, and obtained accurate performance but inconsistent velocities. I assume improvements are continuous with

such a product, but I'm also aware that the product's future is clouded because of litigation.

The Bulk Factor

I wanted to determine how bulk and resulting air space might affect a powder charge's uniformity, so I used an electronic powder scale to weigh 50 test samples of 100-grain charges (by volume) of each powder (See Figure 6-1). Variances are caused by density, moisture content and measuring techniques. I did these tests only to show the difference in powder weights. I don't suggest weighing black powder other than with the volumetric measure designed for the job.

100-Grain Test

What does 100 grains of powder produce in the in-line muzzleloader? Do the various black powders and black-powder substitutes perform significantly different? To answer those questions, I took 10 new in-line muzzleloaders to the range and chronographed 100-grain loads using 10 different black powders and black-powder substitutes (see Figure 6-2). I used a

The Ten-Grain Increment Test			
Bullet	Pyrodex Select Load		
Type	80 grains	90 grains	100 grains
240 XTP	1,490	1,581	1,658
250 XTP	1,465	1,574	1,631
260 KNIGHT	1,452	1,543	1,614

standard 300-grain hollow-point saboted bullet, and a uniform loading technique. I fired five shots of each through an Oehler 35P chronograph placed 10 feet from the muzzle. I cleaned thoroughly between each test by swabbing with solvent-soaked patches and finishing with dry patches.

I also fired one fouling shot before each chronograph string and did not swab between shots during the chronographing.

The rifles I used were the Marlin MLS-50; Peifer TS-93; Remington M700ML; Markesbery Black Bear; the LK-93 Wolverine, MK-85 and DISC Rifle from Knight Rifles; and the Firehawk, Thunderhawk and System 1 rifles from Thompson/Center Arms. All of the rifles were made in the United States.

I selected these rifles because they're all of excellent quality and represent a range of costs and designs. They're also a representative sample of most models sold throughout North America.

For ignition devices, the DISC and TS-93 used 209 shotgun primers. The other eight rifles used standard No. 11 percussion caps.

The Results

What did I find out? The shooting tests revealed a definite difference in velocities generated by 100-grain charges of various black powders and black-powder substitutes. The accompanying chart shows this clearly. (See Figure 6-2).

In addition, some muzzleloading rifles seem to consistently generate slightly higher velocities, and some designs are more susceptible to residue-induced accuracy troubles. Because both factors are influenced by human variables and individual rifle characteristics, I didn't mention brands. I also believe that certain muzzleloaders will shoot faster than other identical models using the same load.

Figure 6-3. How much of a difference does 10 grains mean in terms of velocity? The author found that 10 grains of powder increases velocity more than 100 feet per second. In addition, 10 grains of powder has more significance than 10 grains of bullet weight.

Barrel length was not as important in the results as one might expect. In fact, the Thunderhawk and its 21-inch barrel was consistently one of the faster shooting rifles. Again, though, that might be a factor of the rifle tested.

The 10-Grain Increment

I also tested the significance of varying the powder charge and bullet weight, because these are the primary factors in developing an accurate load. I used several rifles to shoot test loads through the chronograph using charges of 80, 90 and 100 grains of Pyrodex Select with 240-, 250- and 260-grain bullets. The results show that 10 grains of powder has more significance than 10 grains of bullet weight (see Figure 6-3).

Ten additional grains of powder can increase velocities by more than 100 feet per second, which can achieve significant improvements in accuracy. The trick is determining which amount of powder works best with which bullet in your muzzleloader.

Pyrodex Pellets: The Ideal Propellant?

The success and growth of muzzleloading in the 1990s can partially be attributed to the user-friendly virtues surrounding in-line rifles. Shooters can open up a blister-pack that not only contains an in-line rifle, but all of the essential accessories. After a quick review of the enclosed instructions, they can then go to the range and start shooting decent groups.

In terms of "user-friendly," nothing defines

Pyrodex Pellets are made from Pyrodex RS powder compressed into 45-caliber cylinders. They have the most uniform burning characteristics of any propellant the author has tested. The result is uniform velocities and low shot-to-shot variations.

that term more soundly than Pyrodex Pellets. No longer are powder flasks and measuring devices required in muzzleloading. In effect, each pellet is a pre-measured, uniformly compressed charge. Most in-lines shoot great with two Pyrodex Pellets and just about any projectile.

Many manufacturers of in-lines that resemble centerfires suggest using three Pyrodex Pellets and lightweight saboted bullets. Such loads can produce muzzle velocities of 2,000 to 2,100 fps. But increasing the charge from two to three pellets to increase velocity, also increases recoil, smoke and muzzle blast.

Hodgdon warns shooters not to exceed 100 grains equivalent with any projectile combination. With the exception of T/C's new Black Mountain Magnum and the Traditions sidehammer, muzzleloaders do not work well with pellets.

The Origins of Pyrodex Pellets

How did Pyrodex Pellets originate? The men responsible for the pellets are Dean Barrett and Bob Hodgdon. In the early 1980s, Barrett had visited a military arsenal and learned about solid-fuel technology under development for several munitions projects. Hodgdon wondered if his company could develop a solid propellant pellet for muzzleloaders, providing an alternative to granular powder. Barrett and Hodgdon made the first pellets by hand in 1983. Several years later, Barrett was granted patents for the unique product.

Pyrodex Pellets were introduced at the 1996 SHOT Show, and became an immediate success. During 1996-97, demand far outstripped supply. The company's 16-hour shifts involving much hand production struggled to turn out the necessary product.

Many millions of pellets were made and sold. In 1997-98, automated processing helped Hodgdon catch up to the demand. Pyrodex Pellets became available at gunshops throughout the United States and Canada. Pellet sales remain strong, admittedly to a degree at the expense of Pyrodex RS and Pyrodex Select.

The Pyrodex division of Hodgdon Powders is located on an old Air Force base west of Kansas City. The buildings are located in a 65-acre compound that houses offices; mixing, pelletizing, packaging and shipping facilities; material storage; finished-product storage; and a quality-control lab. In addition, a hanger contains a maintenance shop, more finished-product packaging facilities, and bulk storage for the many boxes and containers required to package and ship Pyrodex products.

Making the Pyrodex

How is Pyrodex made? Materials from two buildings are taken into a third building, where they're blended to make Pyrodex. The process is fully automated and controlled via closed-circuit video monitors. The operator sits at a table of knobs, dials, gauges and buttons and watches the TV screens to monitor the job's progress.

He remotely loads and dumps mechanized buckets, moving them from building to building, even giving them a pneumatic thumping to ensure they're completely emptied.

The three key buildings are linked by an overhead system, so all components can be stored separately and mixed in a remote location. No one is allowed inside any of the buildings when the job is taking place, although one designated employee stands by in case anything requires adjustment or repair.

Every container, and even the building itself, is designed to ensure that pressures from fire or explosion are safely released. As the process proceeds, a wet mixture of chemicals is carefully dried and screened, resulting in three grades of Pyrodex: P, RS and Select.

After the Pyrodex is blended, it's placed inside special containers and taken to the pellet-manufacturing building. A wall separates raw Pyrodex materials from the processing area, and the amount of raw material is restricted for safety reasons. Pyrodex powder flows into a uniquely designed machine, and the resulting pellets are stored inside large boxes for eventual packaging. Each new batch of Pyrodex Pellets is tested by quality-control experts to ensure continuity and consistency. By the time the pellets reach individual hunters, they're ready to make shooting more simple and reliable.

Pyrodex Pellets have contributed to the in-line muzzleloader's popularity. Because each pellet is a premeasured, uniformly compressed charge, powder flasks and measuring devices are not required. Beginners can shoot decent groups almost immediately. Shown above are two Rightnour pellet dispensers, which quickly release two pellets when needed.

Using Pyrodex Pellets

Originally, only one pellet design — a 50-grain unit intended for .50- caliber muzzleloaders — was produced and marketed, arriving at stores in plastic boxes of 100. In 1998, Hodgdon added a 30-grain pellet to the line. These pellets were marketed in handy blister packs of 24 units. In 1999, Hodgdon began marketing boxes of 100 pellets of 30-grain size. At the same time, Hodgdon began selling 60-grain pellets for .54-caliber muzzleloaders, as well as 30-grain, .44-caliber pellets for black-powder revolvers.

What advantages do Pyrodex Pellets really offer? I've shot pellets in a variety of muzzleloaders and have chronographed hundreds of rounds through my Oehler 35P. Pellets offer

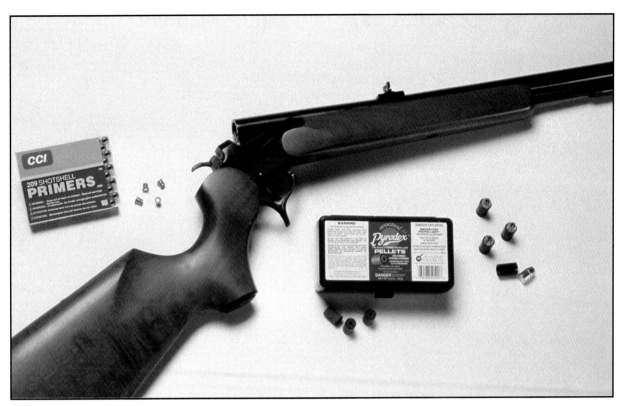

The author finds that most in-lines shoot well with two Pyrodex Pellets and just about any projectile. The author's son, Glen McMurchy, discovered two Pyrodex Pellets shot better groups in his MK-85 than the original black-powder load he had been using. In fact, he used the two-pellet load to kill this huge Saskatchewan white-tailed buck, left.

more uniform velocities, and shot-to-shot variations are usually low because powder compression is not a factor. But note that I did not claim they produce higher velocities. That is by design. Hodgdon intended to retain the original performance characteristics of its popular Pyrodex RS with the new pellets.

How do the pellets perform in the field? I've heard rumors and accusations that pellets are more sensitive to moisture than granular powder. I have not encountered such problems. More than once I've dropped pellets into water, snow or mud and had them ignite perfectly. But I've never had to use pellets that were in prolonged contact with moisture, but I doubt any propellant could perform after such exposure.

During storage, no deterioration should occur if the pellets are kept in a cool, dry location. Even so, I practice with my older powder stocks and hunt with the freshest pellets I can obtain.

I've noticed that the black powder on the ignition end of pellets tends to disappear after they're carried a few days in a speed loader, but this does not cause ignition problems. The black powder is there for insurance, but good ignition will occur whether it's on or off.

Conclusion

Obviously, Pyrodex Pellets will survive long-term only if they function well in the field. Personally, I think they're up to the challenge. My son, Glen, agrees. He recently hunted with Pyrodex Pellets for the first time. Glen had never tried pellets in his old Knight MK-85 until I bugged him about "getting with it" and shooting a modern powder. To his surprise, two pellets shot a better group than his original black-powder load. His first and only shot at game with the pellets brought down a beautiful Saskatchewan white-tailed buck. The deer's rack had a gross score exceeding 178 points, and its net score was just under 168 points. Needless to say, Glen is now a confirmed pellet shooter, although he will never admit I had told him so.

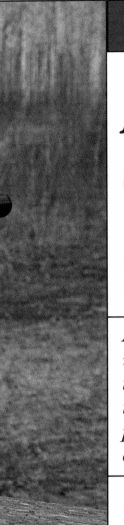

CHAPTER 7

Accuracy Comparisons at the Range

Accuracy is a bottom-line business, and the group of in-line rifles we tested shot very well. Our tests showed that in-line rifles shoot excellent groups right out of the box. Although we shot a variety of bullets and propellants, we found that Pyrodex Pellets and extruded lead hollow-point bullets usually shot best.

Shooting an in-line rifle, particularly a new one, is more complicated than an afternoon at the range with a centerfire rifle. Muzzleloaders consume much more time because every shot must be individually prepared. It also requires some barrel cleaning during the shooting session itself, rather than waiting until after all the shooting is finished.

Because of the more involved, complicated nature of shooting in-lines at the range, shooters should develop a technique or procedure to ensure safe, consistent results. The method you develop should be based on being organized and carrying out each step uniformly time after time.

Let's assume the shooter has obtained all of the basic accesso-ries and components necessary, and that they are neatly stored in an appropriate container. Many shooters use plastic or metal tool-boxes or tackle boxes. I suggest putting essential items into the open lid of the box, if possible, to ensure you can keep track of them. These essentials include the capper, short-starter, 209 primers (if appropriate), bullets, powder flask and measure (or a box of Pyrodex pellets).

Pre-soaked patches are a great time-saver. They can be purchased from various sources such as Hodgdon, or made up by placing a stack of flannel patches into a plastic pudding jar, squirting in some solvent, and letting it sit overnight. Pre-soaked patches should be moist, not dripping wet.

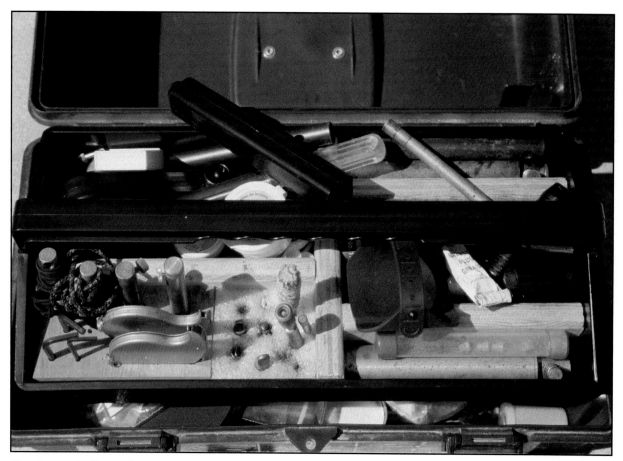

Shooting an in-line at the range requires organization. The author suggests compiling shooting items in a large toolbox. Essential items should be placed in the open tray on top for easy access.

Get into the habit of always placing each component or accessory in the same spot on the bench or in the carrying container. This saves a lot of time and results in safer shooting. Cappers have a nasty habit of disappearing into pockets or under other items, and if you waste time looking for something you've misplaced, it's easy to become forgetful and skip or repeat steps in the loading-and-shooting sequence. Also consider buying a range rod. These one-piece fiberglass or aluminum rods handle the roughest chore, from seating a tight-fitting conical to pulling the same bullet out if you forget the powder charge.

Popping Caps

After organizing your basics on the bench, and placing a target downrange, pop two or three caps or primers to ensure the nipple and breech plug are clear. A great technique is to run a dry patch down the bore and leave the patch and ramrod in the barrel as you snap the caps. This prevents oil from blowing into the barrel, if it was present. In addition, a blackened area on the patch confirms the flame-path is clear. If you don't put the patch into the bore, hold the muzzle near grass or vegetation and watch to ensure the grass or leaves move when you fire caps. When snow is present, hold the muzzle a few inches above loose snow and watch for a puff upon ignition. If nothing moves during such test shots, the flame channel is probably blocked. Use a nipple pick to clear it.

Charging Your In-Line

The next step is charging the rifle. Pour the powder charge into the measuring device, and then pour the powder down the bore. Insert the bullet, whether saboted or conical, into the muzzle and align it as straight as possible. With a smooth stroke of the short-starter, push the bullet into the bore. Frequently, there is resistance as the rifling engraves the sabot or the conical's lead. Once the projectile is pushed down a bit farther, however, it should move smoothly for the length of the short-starter.

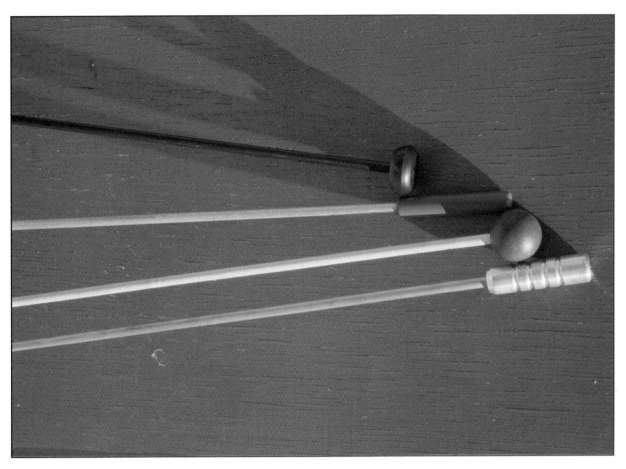

Now switch to the range rod, or ramrod, and again smoothly push the bullet down until feeling resistance.

The final push to seat the bullet atop the powder charge should be as uniform as possible. This push will vary with each shooter, and requires some experimenting. Some shooters quit pushing immediately upon feeling the charge, while others give an extra push or a sharp slap on the end of the ramrod when feeling the bullet bottom out.

After removing the ramrod and pointing the rifle in a safe direction, install the priming device. If using a cap, press it firmly onto the nipple, but don't mash it on with lots of force. Now you're ready to shoot. Frequently, the first shot on the range will be slightly outside the group, because there might be some oil in the bore. This tendency can be minimized by running one or two dry patches through the barrel before firing.

Swabbing for Accuracy

After the shot, swab the bore. Although this is not practical in most hunting situations, swabbing will almost always improve the rifle's

In-line shooters should consider buying a one-piece fiberglass or aluminum ramrod for the range. They are usually stronger than standard factory-supplied ramrods, and are excellent for seating and pulling tight-fitting bullets.

accuracy. Swabbing will also leave the bore more closely resembling its condition for the first — and, usually, only — shot you'll get at a whitetail. In addition, removing the residue ensures easier bullet seating when reloading.

Swabbing during practice usually requires some experimentation and personal decisions to determine how much bore cleaning is necessary. The minimum is a "spit-patch," whereby you simply moisten a patch with saliva before pushing it down the bore. I prefer pre-soaked patches, but I also use spit-patches in a pinch. One simple tip for swabbing: Always push the moistened patch down the bore in short jabs. Don't swab as if you're seating a bullet. The jabbing action ensures the jag and patch don't accumulate a big "wedge" of residue that jams the rod at the bottom of the stroke.

Although swabbing is essential to accuracy and performance, it is not a science. It requires

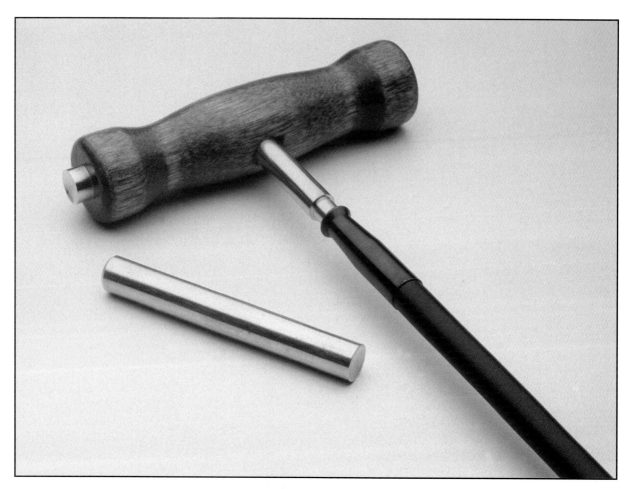

some trial and error. Some powders require more swabbing than others, and some barrels respond differently to swabbing than others. I frequently push a solvent-soaked patch down the bore, withdraw it and turn it over before making the second pass. If the swabs are too moist, a dry patch follow-up might be necessary. The key to swabbing is to remove accumulated fouling without leaving too much moisture in the bore to contaminate the powder charge and cause a hang-fire or dud charge.

Range shooting is the time to experiment and find which procedures and components produce peak accuracy in your in-line. Each rifle makes its own rules, so don't expect your rifle to shoot its best with your buddy's favorite load. The more shooting on the range, the greater your confidence when you go on your next hunt.

Out-of-the-Box Accuracy

How well do in-line muzzleloaders shoot, and what kind of groups should you expect from out-of-the-box rifles? Also, how much better

After charging your in-line rifle, insert the bullet and align it as straight as possible, right. Use a short starter, such as Thompson/Center Arms' T-Handle, above, to push the bullet down the bore. Finish pushing and seating the bullet with a range rod.

can a "pro" rifleman shoot than average in-line buyers. Does fine-tuning help accuracy? Those are some of the questions shooters ask after they buy their first in-line rifle.

Some time ago, my friends and I test-fired 10 new in-lines to determine how accurately they shot right out of the box. We tightened stock bolts, installed Weaver style bases, cleaned the barrels, and began preparing a variety of powder and bullet combinations. By using Warne Maxima detachable scope rings, we could quickly mount the Nikon 3-9X Monarch scopes we used for the tests. I only had to loosen one ring to adjust the mounting distance between rifle actions.

We set each scope at 9X for the tests, and used a bore-sighter to minimize the number of sighting-in shots required each time we remounted a scope on a different rifle. All

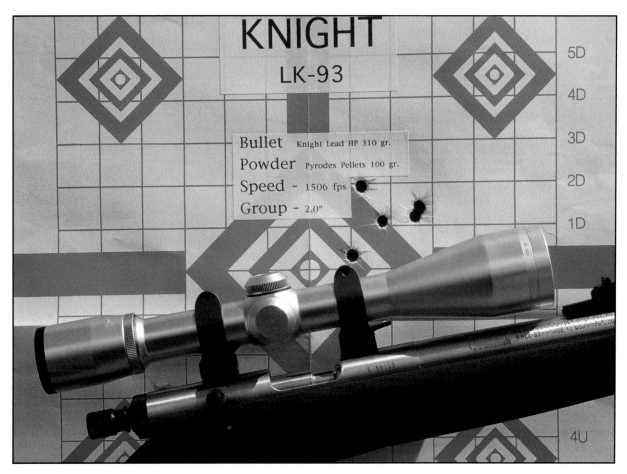

KNIGHT
LK-93

Bullet   Knight Lead HP 310 gr.
Powder   Pyrodex Pellets 100 gr.
Speed - 1506 fps
Group - 2.0"

5D
4D
3D
2D
1D
4U

Range shooting is the time to experiment and find which procedures and components produce peak accuracy. Moreover, honing your marksmanship skills at the range will give you greater confidence on your next hunt.

shooting was done with two-man teams at 100 yards from commercial bench-rest pedestals and sandbags. Each rifle was checked at 25 yards and then zeroed at 100 yards, which was usually done in five or six shots. Then we shot a standard group of loads to determine the rifle's best accuracy. We used standard targets sold by Modern Muzzleloading. These pink and gray targets work great for scope and open-sight shooting. We also marked and measured all groups. At first we used three-shot groups to determine the loads that each rifle appeared to shoot well. When we determined accurate loads, we fired five-shot tests. Because some muzzleloading manufacturers also market bullets for their rifles, we shot "dedicated" bullets when relevant. The favorite loads for most rifles used 90 or 100 grains of powder.

We fired black powder and Pyrodex with conical and saboted bullets. We swabbed with two patches between each group (except with

FFg and FFFG, when more swabbing was required). We moistened the patches with a black-powder solvent and let them sit overnight in a sealed container so they were of uniform dampness. We experienced significant differences in velocity if the swabs were too moist, so we took care to use consistently moist patches.

We found that many rifles shot very accurately with conical bullets. We used Buffalo Bullets, Big Bore Express and T/C Maxi slugs with excellent results. These are hard hitting bullets that shoot well with heavy powder loads.

Our shooters were experienced riflemen with decades of competitive shooting experience. Each "pro" fired three 3-shot groups with each rifle and its most accurate load. I then asked two "average" hunters to shoot an identical set of targets to compare their ability with the pros.

Shooting Summaries

What follows is a brief description of each test rifle, and a summary of the shooting tests and results.

Knight LK-93 Wolverine

The LK-93 we tested came in a blister pack, complete with most accessories required to start muzzleloading. I've found that Knight sabots and bullets are perfectly matched to its rifles and almost always deliver exceptional accuracy.

Accuracy Test A

Bullet: Knight Lead, 310 grains
Powder: Two Pyrodex Pellets, 100 grains
Velocity: 1,515 fps
"Expert" group average: 1.33 inches
"Hunter" group average: 2.46 inches

Accuracy Test B

Bullet: Knight Red Hot, 300 grains
Powder: Pyrodex Select, 100 grains
Velocity: 1,544 fps
"Expert" group average: 1.53 inches
"Hunter" group average: 2.75 inches

Knight DISC Rifle

The DISC (Dual Ignition System Concept) Rifle is the marquee model in the Knight Rifles line. This bolt-action is on the top shelf of in-line rifles.

Accuracy Test A

Bullet: Knight Red Hot, 250 grains
Powder: Pellets 150 grains
Velocity: 2,075 fps
"Expert" group average: 1.03 inches
"Hunter" group average: 1.75 inches

Accuracy Test B

Bullet: Knight Red Hot, 250 grains
Powder: RS 150 grains
Velocity: 1,890 fps
"Expert" group average: 1.5 inches
"Hunter" group average: 1.74 inches

Marlin MLS-50

The Marlin MLS-50 is similar to the original T/C Firehawk in appearance. The Marlin MLS-50 is a great-handling rifle.

Accuracy Test A

Bullet: Knight Lead, 310 grains
Powder: Two Pyrodex Pellets, 100 grains
Velocity: 1,500 fps
"Expert" group average: 2.63 inches
"Hunter" Group Average: 3.88 inches

Accuracy Test B

Bullet: Knight Red Hot, 250 grains
Powder: Select 100 grains
Velocity: 1,549 fps
"Expert" group average: 2 inches
"Hunter" group average: 2.95 inches

Remington M700 ML Blued

The M700ML is based on one of the best-selling bolt-action centerfire rifles in history. This is a nicely built rifle, but it has a distinct muzzle-heavy feel.

Accuracy Test A

Bullet: Remington JHP, 303 grains
Powder: Two Pyrodex Pellets, 100 grains
Velocity: 1,533 fps
"Expert" group average: 1.31 inches
"Hunter" group average: 2.88 inches

Accuracy Test B

Bullet: Remington JHP, 275 grains
Powder: Select 100 grains
Velocity: 1,414 fps
"Expert" group average: 1.23 inches
"Hunter" group average: 3.05 inches

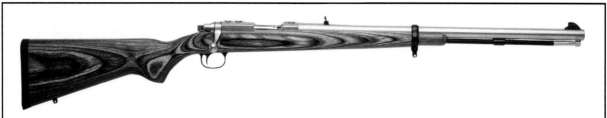

Ruger 77/50

The Ruger in-line rifle is a nice-handling bolt-action with typical Ruger quality.
This rifle was designed with the deer hunter in mind.

Accuracy Test A

Bullet: Knight Lead HP, 310 grains
Powder: Two Pyrodex Pellets, 100 grains
Velocity: 1,501 fps
"Expert" group average: 1.62 inches
"Hunter" group average: 2.76 inches

Accuracy Test B

Bullet: Knight Lead HP, 260 grains
Powder: Select 100 grains
Velocity: 1,724 fps
"Expert" group average: 1.75 inches
"Hunter" group average: 2.75 inches

Traditions Lightning

The Lightning bolt-action in-line is a reliable, accurate rifle. The Lightning offers typical
Traditions value and more options than any other in-line.

Accuracy Test A

Bullet: Knight Lead HP, 310 grains
Powder: Two Pyrodex Pellets, 100 grains
Velocity: 1,544 fps
"Expert" group average: 2.89 inches
"Hunter" group average: 3.80 inches

Accuracy Test B

Bullet: Barnes HP, 250 grains
Powder: Three Pyrodex Pellets, 150 grains
Velocity: 2,024 fps
"Expert" group average: 3.00 inches
"Hunter" group average: 3.95 inches

Thompson/Center Arms' Black Diamond

The T/C Black Diamond is a well-designed in-line rifle that quickly became a hot seller after its introduction in the late 1990s. T/C had to hustle to make them fast enough to meet consumer demand.

Accuracy Test A

Bullet: T/C "XTP," 300 grains
Powder: Two Pyrodex Pellets, 100 grains
Velocity: 1,602 fps
"Expert" group average: 1.03 inches
"Hunter" group average: 2.88 inches

Accuracy Test B

Bullet: Barnes, 250 grains
Powder: Select 100 grains
Velocity: 1,570 fps
"Expert" group average: 1.60 inches
"Hunter" group average: 2.65 inches

Thompson/Center Arms' Encore 209x50

This break-open rifle was arguably the best in-line value on the market as the 1900s ended. It offers versatility unmatched by any other design. On top of that, it is superbly accurate.

Accuracy Test A

Bullet: T/C "PTX," 250 grains
Powder: Three Pyrodex Pellets, 150 grains
Velocity: 2,045 fps
"Expert" group average: 1.00 inches
"Hunter" group average: 1.58 inches

Accuracy Test B

Bullet: Barnes, 250 grains
Powder: Three Pyrodex Pellets, 150 grains
Velocity: 2,130 fps
"Expert" group average: 0.90 inches
"Hunter" group average: 1.25 inches

CVA HunterBolt

The HunterBolt is a moderately priced bolt-action in-line rifle that offers many features for deer hunters. This rifle handles very well and performs in fine fashion.

Accuracy Test A

Bullet: Knight Lead HP, 310 grain
Powder: Two Pyrodex Pellets, 100 grains
Velocity: 1,499 fps
"Expert" group average: 3.33 inches
"Hunter" group average: 3.93 inches

Accuracy Test B

Bullet: Barnes HP, 250 grains
Powder: Three Pyrodex Pellets, 150 grains
Velocity: 2,088 fps
"Expert" group average: 3.05 inches
"Hunter" group average: 4.66 inches

Kahnke Model 94

The Model 94 is a blued-steel and walnut-stock in-line that resembles a Winchester 94, but without the lever. A solid, simple design makes this a user-friendly muzzleloader.

Accuracy Test A

Bullet: Knight Red Hot, 300 grains
Powder: Select 100 grains
Velocity: 1,506 fps
"Expert" group average: 1.92 inches
"Hunter" group average: 3.63 inches

Accuracy Test B

Bullet: Knight Lead HP, 260 grains
Powder: Select 100 grains
Velocity: 1,801 fps
"Expert" group average: 1.48 inches
"Hunter" group average: 2.35 inches

In one month, the author chronographed more than 800 shots while testing in-line rifles. Wayward sabots often struck and damaged the plastic light diffusers despite attempts to protect them.

The Results

Accuracy is a bottom-line business, and the group of in-lines we tested shot very well. During the tests, we tried to eliminate as many variables as possible. One of the toughest factors to control is the human element. For example, what if someone just isn't having a great day? For what it's worth, however, all of the shooters who participated in these tests were satisfied with their personal performance.

The results indicated that the "pros" shot groups at least 50 percent smaller than those fired by average shooters. Technically speaking, of course, my data are not scientifically defendable. For one, the sample size might not be large enough to mean anything statistically. But it was still an interesting test.

The tests also showed that in-line rifles shoot very well out of the box. The charts also show that we fired a wide variety of bullets, powders and charges. For what it's worth, however, we found the pellets and the simple, extruded lead hollow-point bullets usually shot best.

The Oehler chronographs worked perfectly through all of this shooting. In one month, we chronographed more than 800 shots. (I had a protective baffle in place to protect the body of the first screen, but wayward sabots often struck all three plastic light diffusers. A tube of Crazy-Glue in my kit helped patch the diffusers, which helped them last for the entire test.

For continuity, we had one scorer with a Mitotoyo dial caliper measure all the groups.

Swabbing vs. No-Swabbing

After this shooting test, we decided to investigate the impact that loading technique has on accuracy. We reshot the test without any swabbing between each shot during the three-shot string. We simply ran a couple of moist patches down each bore after every test, and then dried with one plain patch. Unfortunately, we could not draw any conclusion, other than the fact the barrels were a lot dirtier and more difficult to clean. Accuracy varied. Some rifles shot slightly better and others shot worse. Velocities also varied so much that I'm reluc-

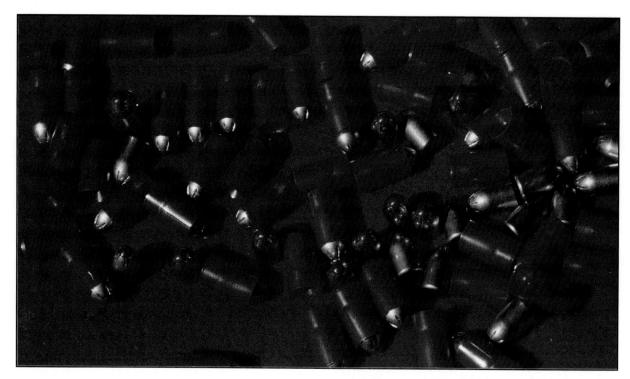

tant to draw conclusions. We detected a tendency in some rifles for velocity to increase as the bore fouled, but others showed no significant difference. Overall, we did not see any radical declines or improvements in accuracy/velocity in dirty barrels. Perhaps three shots is not enough of a test for any variables to show up, but because we're interested only in scenarios that relate to hunting accuracy, we did not shoot larger samples.

When discussing these tests with Tony Knight, I asked what he considered the most common accuracy problems. He cited inconsistent loading procedures and failure to consistently swab. Then he brought up a situation many in-line shooters never consider. Allowing a barrel to overheat, by a combination of rapid shooting sequences and practicing during intense summer heat, causes plastic sabots to soften, which causes inaccuracy. Knight says Modern Muzzleloading Inc. frequently gets calls from shooters who complain that their third or fourth shot seems to stray significantly from the group. This only occurs during extremely warm shooting conditions, and is likely related to sabot failure. The solution is obvious.

Mid-Morning Outfitters Accuracy

My son, Glen, and I always compete to see whose rifle shoots best. One afternoon many years ago we met my buddy Chopper near his

According to Tony Knight, founder of Knight Rifles, rapid shooting sequences in hot weather can overheat the barrel, which in turn softens plastic sabots and causes inaccuracy. This might explain why the third or fourth shot can stray from the group when shooting in hot weather.

local rifle range. This was just before one of our Mid-Morning Outfitters hunts. Because deer season was near, Chopper was shooting his Knight MK-85 in-line as much as possible. When we drove up, Glen asked Chopper what size groups he was shooting.

"About an inch," Chopper replied.

Glen and I had been shooting hundreds of shots a week at that time, and our three-shot groups reflected all of this practice. Glen's pet MK-85 carbine was shooting superb groups, and he had recently begun breaking the magical 1-inch mark for five shots at 100 yards. My son was impressed when our partner casually said he was also shooting 1-inch groups. Unfortunately, Chopper then blew it when he mentioned that his groups consisted of two shots at 20 yards!

CHAPTER 8

Sight Systems for In-line Muzzleloaders

No firearm will shoot to its potential without good sights. Not all sights are created equal, however, in quality or performance. In addition, the vagaries of personal preference are particularly obvious when choosing sights and riflescopes.

After answering questions about which muzzleloader to buy and which caliber is best for deer hunting, the next most commonly asked question is this: "Which scope should I buy for my new in-line muzzleloader?"

Of course, the questions never totally cease. After discussing scopes, you'll often hear, "What accessories do I need to get this thing shooting?" or "How do I load this thing — again?" And then, finally, there is this question: "How do I clean this thing?"

No doubt those are all valid questions, and there is no absolutely right or wrong answer to any of them. What works for one shooter might fail miserably for his buddy. The vagaries of personal preference are particularly obvious when the topic is sights and riflescopes.

Which Sights to Choose

No firearm will shoot to its potential without good sights. Not all sights are created equal, however, in quality or performance. One significant factor influences which sights to consider for muzzleloaders, and it has nothing to do with personal preference: government regulations. In some states, wildlife agencies restrict which sights can be used on muzzleloaders during black-powder seasons. This is of primary importance when deciding to replace or upgrade factory open sights on your muzzleloader. Several states do not allow telescopic sights of any kind, while several allow only non-magnifying scopes. In addition, some jurisdictions do not allow laser or electronic sights.

Such regulations are constantly being reviewed and are subject to

Modern Muzzleloading Photo

Fiber-optic sight systems are easier to see and use than traditional iron sights, and many in-line companies now offer them as standard equipment. Most systems employ two fiber-optic rods in the rear sight, and one in place of the front bead. This creates the image of three glowing dots in the shooter's sight picture.

change. The trend in the late 1990s, however, was to relax regulations and allow the use of optics. Suffice to say, it is the hunter's responsibility to be aware of the regulations wherever he happens to be.

Most muzzleloaders come out of the box with open sights, although a few in-lines have been marketed with no sights on the barrels. Flip-up sights and plain posts were common for years. Unfortunately, sights have long been an item where factories cut corners, possibly because some shooters discard them in favor of scopes. Some in-lines use plastic open sights, but they simply do not stand up to rugged use.

Another pet peeve of mine is that too many in-line rifles arrive from the factory with loose sights. I frequently see sight screws that were not tightened properly or even checked.

During a visit to the Thompson/Center factory, however, I was impressed with its methods for sighting in open sights. Essentially,

T/C uses a laser beam to align the sights. The operator installs the in-line into a fixture, and adjusts the sights in whatever direction the monitor indicates. This technique is state-of-the-art and incredibly accurate. This technology eliminates the need to shoot each rifle to adjust its sights.

Amazing Modern Sights

In the late 1990s, most in-line manufacturers switched to fiber-optic designs for their standard-issue open sights. I believe these are the best open sights ever placed on hunting rifles. Fiber-optic sights have come a long way in a short time, becoming more rugged and superbly user-friendly. The most common design employs the simple job of aligning three glowing dots horizontally. Two green dots are located on both sides of the rear sight notch, and a bright red dot is located on the tip of the front post.

Hunters can use these sights in two basic ways. Some prefer to place the red front-sight dot on the target and then align the red dot between the two green rear-sight dots. Others prefer to set the three dots in line and then put the red dot on the target. Either way gives you perfect sight alignment. The glowing dots make for extremely fast, accurate shooting.

The author likes the simple design and performance of the Ashley Outdoors Aperture Ghost-Ring. The large rear peep hole and large white post atop the muzzle are rugged and easy to use.

Another great sight for muzzleloaders is the Ashley Outdoors Aperture Ghost-Ring. This is a compact, super-rugged aperture sight with an oversized peep-hole, combined with a large, highly visible white front post. The concept is simple: line up the big white post on the target and shoot. Your eye naturally centers itself through the big aperture and aiming becomes instinctive. In fact, the shooter isn't even aware of the rear sight. The company also offers a rear sight that fits onto Weaver scope bases. This allows hunters to switch to open sights quickly when required, as when hunting in a state that doesn't allow scopes, or in the rare case when a scope fails. Are these sights accurate? Amazingly so.

A variety of aftermarket sights can be installed on in-lines, but most in-line owners are most interested in telescopic sights. Many set up their in-Line with a scope that can quickly and reliably be detached and reattached, depending on regulations and circumstances.

Although riflescopes make good sense on in-lines, you should also consider a couple of other optical sights. "Red-dot" sights offered by several manufacturers work great on in-lines. These small, rugged little units are extremely fast to aim because your eye can quickly acquire the bright red dot and place it on the target. I've hunted with red-dot scopes and found them ideal for shots out to 75 yards or so. Most red-dot units have dials that control the dot's brightness and allow for pinpoint zeroing adjustments. The T/C, Millett and Simmons red-dot scopes I use appear to share similar ancestry, and they're reliable hunting tools.

The other alternative to riflescopes is one of my all-time favorite sights, the Bushnell Holosight. The Holosight's technology creates the slickest, fastest sight on the market. How accurate is its floating dot? I once removed the Holosight from a Knight in-line rifle and installed it on a super-accurate .308 Winchester target rifle. Several shooters then proceeded to shoot five-shot groups at 100 yards that were at or under the 1-inch mark. Such accuracy is more than adequate for muzzleloaders. The Holosight is foolproof and takes little effort to master. The dial adjustments are accurate and

Red-dot 1X scopes are accurate, fast to aim, and work well in low-light conditions. The author finds them ideal for shots out to 75 yards.

easy to zero. As with the red-dot, the only concern with this modern wonder is that if you forget to turn off the power, you'll kill batteries. I've used the Holosight under various conditions and have never had a problem shooting quickly and accurately. Running deer at "real-close" range are doable with the Holosight, and "real close" is the only moving shot I take with muzzleloaders.

Riflescopes are Justified

Although open sights and non-magnifying optics allow quick, accurate shots, most in-lines can shoot accurately at distances that justify the higher magnification and finer-aiming reticles of riflescopes. At ranges farther than 100 yards, I find that most open sights and aperture sights are too coarse for shots at deer. Holdover becomes difficult. Another consideration is that older eyes start to have real problems focusing on two sights and a target. Scopes are necessary, logical tools that enable shooters to get the most performance out of their in-lines.

When considering a scope for your in-line, analyze when and where most of your hunting and shooting will occur. Muzzleloaders are shot many more times at the rifle range than at deer. Because you want your in-line to shoot as accurately as possible, remember that you can hold more accurately with a higher-power scope than a lower-power scope off the bench. In other words, you'll shoot tighter groups at 100 yards with a 9X scope than with a 3X model. When at the range perfecting loads and mastering the intricacies of in-line muzzleloaders, I suggest a medium-range variable hunting scope in 2-7X or 3-9X range. For years, Tony Knight recommended 4X scopes for his rifles, and I agree with that for hunting. Any scope is better than no scope. But for all-around use, I prefer the 3-9X, and hunt with it set at 4X or 5X. At the range, I always shoot targets with the scope set on its highest power.

Let your hunting area dictate the power range, using low power in heavy cover where close-range shooting is the norm. Reserve higher magnifications for hunting more open terrain, especially when you have time to boost the magnification after spotting deer at a distance.

Choose and Spend Wisely

For unknown reasons, many hunters think they don't need to spend as much money on a scope for their muzzleloader as they do on a scope for a centerfire rifle. This lack of logic escapes me. Hunting is hunting, regardless of the rifle underneath the scope. I want the best optics available at all times when I'm deer hunting. Although in-lines don't shoot as far as centerfires, there's no valid reason to cut back on scope quality.

Scope mounts for in-line rifles are usually similar to those used for centerfires. I prefer high-quality detachable mounts that allow me to remove the scope each time I clean the rifle. I have total confidence that the Warne, Talley and Leupold detachable mounts on my in-lines will always return to zero. Another advantage of detachable mounts is that they quickly allow the use of metallic sights in the rare occurrence that a scope becomes damaged or fogged.

They're also great for hunters who travel to states that have differing regulations on optics. Although detachable scope mounts are more expensive, they're well worth considering for in-lines.

Most in-line rifles can shoot accurately at distances that justify the higher magnification of riflescopes. Beyond 100 yards, the author finds open-sight systems too coarse for most deer hunting.

Sighting in the In-Line

Sighting in a new in-line rifle can be frustrating for shooters who are entering the sport. The fact that they have never shot these rifles before makes life more complicated. The smoke, noise and loading procedure are mildly disconcerting. On top of all this, the scope must be zeroed so that load-testing can begin. Fortunately, there's a simple technique to sighting in that makes life much easier. I call it the "two-shot sighting-in system."

First, shoot at short range so you're certain to hit the target. The larger the target the better, but don't set it past 20 yards. Second, with the rifle well-rested, fire one shot. If you hit the target someplace, proceed. If you missed, move the target closer or get someone else to shoot! Once you're on the paper, you're ready to move on.

Remove the scope's turret caps. Put the rifle back in the rest and place the cross-hairs on

the original aiming mark. WITHOUT MOVING THE RIFLE, carefully move the alignment screws to "track" the cross-hairs over to the bullet hole. Once the cross-hairs are superimposed on the impact point, the rifle is zeroed at that distance.

Most importantly, the windage is now very close. Because the bullet crosses the line of sight not far from the end of the barrel, a close-in zero will usually put you close enough at 100 yards so you can fine-tune the scope settings. Tracking the cross-hairs to the bullet hole will also work at 100 yards.

Zeroing Your In-Line Muzzleloader

At what distance should you zero your in-line rifle? The answer depends on many variables. First, how competently do you shoot? Obviously, some hunters can accurately shoot farther than others. Second, are you using a scope or open sights? Obviously, scopes should be zeroed for longer shooting opportunities than open sights. Third, which load are you

The author is impressed with Bushnell's Holosight, above. This high-tech sight superimposes a lighted ring-and-dot image, right, in the sight picture that is accurate and quick to aim.

shooting? Heavy, slow-moving conicals should be zeroed differently than fast, lightweight saboted bullets. Also, consider the average shooting distances you'll likely encounter where you hunt. In addition, you must also consider your rifle's inherent accuracy.

Most hunters should sight in scoped in-lines to hit roughly three inches high at 100 yards. This gives a point-blank range where holding on the deer's chest will be fatal out to about 125 yards. A hold on or slightly below the backline will be fatal out to 150 or 160 yards, depending on the load. Given a 3-inch high zero at 100 yards, slow, heavy bullets will drop about eight inches at 150 yards; while lighter, faster bullets will only drop half that amount, or even less. At 200 yards, slow bullets will be two feet low and the faster ones will drop about 15 inches. As you can see, knowledge of

Which magnification should you choose for a muzzle-loading riflescope? The author prefers a variable scope. At the range, he usually uses the highest magnification setting to sight in, but then uses 4X and 5X for most whitetail hunting situations. Above is the Simmons Aetec scope, which is ideal for in-line muzzleloading.

your trajectory is crucial for shots past 100 yards.

For open sights, sight in so the bullet hits slightly high at 100 yards, but their maximum range will not be much more than 125 yards for most hunters.

What accuracy should you expect at average sighting-in distances? With open sights on an in-line, you should be able to place three shots into a 6- to 10-inch circle at 100 yards. Remember, a deer's vital area is at least a 12- to 15-inch sphere between and behind the front legs. Scoped in-lines should group three shots into a 3- to 4-inch circle or less. The scope makes the difference.

Be sure to practice with your field load and exactly determine your personal killing range.

While shooting to determine your effective range, learn the trajectory at key ranges out to that distance. In other words, if you can consistently shoot a 6- to 7-inch group at 200 yards, learn where your bullet is tracking at 50, 100 and 150 yards so you can be confident out to your 200-yard maximum. I am not suggesting everyone try shots out to 200 yards, but I'm confident in saying that a decent shooting in-line can be deadly at that distance.

Scope Protection

Most in-lines spray caustic residue onto the underside of scopes as each shot is fired. Remove this residue each time you clean the rifle or the scope's finish will be destroyed. Several manufacturers sell nifty vinyl scope protectors that are held in position with velcro. Another solution is applying a few strips of electrician's tape to the scope's underside directly above the action. Always clean scope mounts by wiping and brushing. If you don't clean them regularly, the corrosive residues will cause rust and might freeze the screws.

100-Yard Shooting Tests

Type of Sight	Average Accuracy: 3-Shot Groups — 10 Shooters									
	Test 1	Test 2	Test 3	Test 4	Test 5	Test 6	Test 7	Test 8	Test 9	Test 10
Open Sight:	8.8"	10.2"	13.0"	9.0"	8.6"	7.2"	6.8"	11.8"	5.1"	5.3"
Aperture Sight:	7.0"	8.3"	11.2"	7.6"	7.1"	5.0"	4.0"	10.5"	3.0"	2.6"
Scope Sight:	5.8"	5.0"	6.4"	5.0"	4.1"	3.4"	3.1"	4.8"	3.2"	2.7"
Holosight:	5.3"	6.3"	8.5"	6.0"	6.2"	5.2"	5.6"	5.0"	2.2"	4.0"
Redot Sight:	7.1"	7.0"	9.2"	6.2"	8.1"	7.4"	7.2"	7.1"	4.3"	5.3"

Average Group Size from the Shooting Tests:

Open Sights: 8.6 inches
Aperture Sights: 6.6 inches
Scope Sights: 4.4 inches
Holosight: 5.4 inches
Redot Sight: 6.9 inches

Evaluation of Muzzleloader Sights

With the help of some friends, I conducted a test comparing muzzleloader sighting systems (see Figure 8-1). We shot standard 100-yard targets and full size deer silhouettes from distances of 40 yards to almost 200 yards. We used five new scoped in-lines and five sidehammers fitted with various open and aperture style sights. Three of my sidehammer rifles had aperture sights (Ashley Outdoors Ghost-Ring aperture sights on two, and a Williams peep on the other), one had a folding Williams open sight, and the last one had a no-name set of open sights. I also used a pair of Green Mountain replacement barrels that had standard Modern Muzzleloading open sights.

To extend the test, we also shot the in-lines with their factory-installed open sights, and with a backup aperture sight from Ashley Outdoors that mounted on Weaver scope bases. We also had to replace the original front sights with sights of a more appropriate height on the sidehammer rifles. For that, I used the excellent white blade front sights that Ashley Outdoors recommends for use with its Ghost Ring rear sights.

The in-line rifles all used Weaver bases, and I

Figure 8-1: The author tested various sighting systems by shooting at 100-yard targets and measuring the three-shot group average for each shooter.

used Nikon Monarch (3-9X) and Simmons Aetec (2½-8X) riflescopes in Warne Maxima detachable rings. These variable scopes are great for muzzleloaders. We shot test targets at 9X and reduced the power to 4X or 5X for hunting. We also shot with a Millet SP2 Redot scope and a Bushnell Holosight, both of which were mounted on Weaver bases. The detachable mounts made scope mounting quick and easy.

We used Redfield sighting-in targets for the scopes at 100 yards, and 7-inch black circles for the open sights. We also cut full-sized deer targets out of large sheets of heavy cardboard and mounted them on movable wooden stands. I used head-on and broadside photos of large whitetails to trace lifelike silhouettes.

After much preparation, we started the test shooting. I used hunting loads composed of 300-grain lead saboted bullets and two 50-grain Pyrodex Pellets for the in-lines, and 100 grains of Pyrodex RS in the sidehammer rifles with 370-grain Maxi Balls. We swabbed between each shot, and fired three-shot groups per

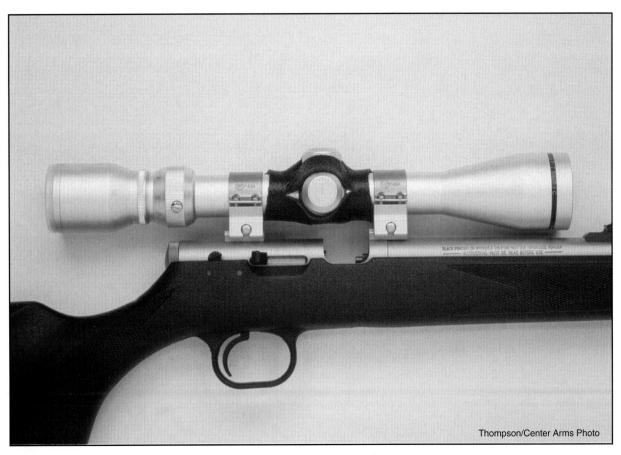

Thompson/Center Arms Photo

shooter at the 100-yard targets.

In a nutshell, to no one's surprise, scoped in-lines outshot open-sighted sidehammers by a significant margin on the range. Most participants preferred to shoot the in-lines. The Redot and Holosight held their own, particularly the Holosight, as some groups matched those of the scoped rifles. Overall, the optical sights cut group size by up to 50 percent for most shooters.

Field Shooting Tests

The field shooting involved one shot per each rifle/sight combination at three silhouettes placed at 40, 90 and 180 yards. Each shooter was told the trajectory to expect for the load in each rifle (its zero location, and bullet drop at 50, 100 and 200 yards). Each shooter shot from a position that might be used while hunting — standing for close-range shots and kneeling or sitting for longer shots. No rests were allowed for the first go-around, but then we shot again using Underwood shooting sticks or a Harris bipod.

Hunting accuracy was determined by shots striking the kill zone. Any shot outside the zone was considered a miss. This was done to

Many in-line rifles spray caustic residue onto the underside of a scope during firing, which can damage a scope's finish. Scope protectors, such as this one from Thompson/Center Arms, help prevent such damage.

facilitate quantifying accuracy. I realize some shots outside the kill zone would cause fatal wounding.

To no one's surprise, the rested shots delivered perfect killing accuracy with the scoped rifles at all ranges. The little Redot and Holosight scopes delivered surprising accuracy at each range: 100 percent accuracy at 40 and 90 yards, and 90 percent accuracy at 180 yards.

The rifles with Ashley ghost ring sights also scored perfect kills at 40 and 90 yards, but most shooters declined shots at 180 yards, while 30 percent of the shots fired at 180 yards struck killing locations. The open sights scored perfect kills at 40 yards, and 90 percent at 90 yards. No shooters tried the 180-yard shot.

What did we learn from this exercise? Scoped rifles outshot apertures and open sights. Any deer standing out to 100 yards was "killable" with any of rifle/sight combinations. We also confirmed that long shots should only be tried by experienced shooters firing from a

Before hunters can estimate bullet drop for long-range shots, they must know the target's distance. Laser rangefinders address this problem, and the author considers them a significant aid for in-line hunters. The laser rangefinders above, from left, are the Bushnell Yardage Pro 1000 and 600, and Nikon's 800.

good rest, and then only if the range and trajectory are known. Shooters were split on the speed of target acquisition, with most agreeing the ghost ring and scopes (particularly the Holosight) were faster to get on target than open sights.

Shooting in the Wind

All of those shooting tests were conducted under nearly ideal conditions, so I made an effort to shoot my favorite hunting loads during strong winds. Suffice to say, even "fast" muzzleloader loads (250-grain Barnes X saboted bullets propelled by three 50-grain Pyrodex Pellets) encounter serious wind drifting. At 200 yards, my bullets drifted almost two feet in winds gusting an estimated 15 mph to 20 mph. Even at 100 yards, the lighter bullets drifted about four inches. I shot some big 520-grain Black Belt bullets at 100 yards, and found they only drifted two inches.

All of this points out two key elements of long-range shooting: knowing your trajectory and range and understanding what wind will do to your bullet. Although I have shot my in-lines at extreme ranges, I much prefer the challenge and satisfaction of a clean kill at ranges as close as possible. Muzzleloaders will kill at surprisingly long distances, but they are devastating at close range.

Although the in-line muzzleloader has developed into a popular hunting tool, most hunters are not sure where their bullets will hit at various distances. However, before hunters even start thinking about bullet drop for longer shots, they must know the target's distance. Laser rangefinders address that question.

I think laser rangefinders are one of the

Not surprisingly, the author, above, found that magnifying riflescopes were the most accurate sighting system. Magnifying scopes and red-dot scopes were also faster to aim than open sights, but he found open sights adequate on deer out to 100 yards.

most significant developments I've seen for hunters in many years. These rangefinders are extremely helpful for muzzleloading hunters, because most bullets have looping trajectories over relatively short distances. Some bullets drop more than eight inches as they travel from 100 to 150 yards. This can be the difference between a hit and a miss on a whitetail.

Most hunters seem to think rangefinders are used to "laser" a buck so they know exactly how far away it is. That rarely happens. Deer seldom stand around and let themselves be laser-ranged. Instead, field-savvy hunters use their laser rangefinders to determine key distances they can readily identify from the blind or tree stand.

Use the rangefinder to laser easily seen rocks, trees, posts or whatever will immediately give a quick reference point if a deer shows up. We use our laser rangefinders when we first look over a spot. We then usually put them away and rely on binoculars to spot game.

Conclusion

Obviously, no hunter can shoot accurately if the rifle sights aren't properly aligned and if he is unsure of his bullet's trajectory. Two factors, skill and knowledge, combine to make successful shots. Although I prefer to shoot as close as possible, I'm confident I can make killing shots out to 200 yards with my in-lines. I have that confidence, but prefer to see the whites of their eyes.

CHAPTER 9

Deadly Bullets for Whitetails

Muzzleloading rifles are devastating on whitetails, but shooters must do their part to find the best load for their rifle. I recommend bullet weights no lighter than 200 grains, with the optimum weight being 250 grains. Within that range, there are countless possibilities. Never before have black-powder hunters had such a variety of bullets to choose from.

Gregg Ritz from Thompson/Center Arms loves to hunt white-tailed deer. Gregg also enjoys tinkering with T/C in-lines, and his job allows him to field-test each new design before it's introduced to North America's deer hunters.

A few years ago, Gregg was on such a hunt on the Nail Ranch near Albany, Texas. Gregg and his guide and good buddy Calvin were seeing lots of bucks but nothing caught Gregg's fancy. At least until one rattling session turned up a dandy 6-by-6. Gregg wanted that buck for his wall!

Unfortunately, there were three problems. First, the buck and several does were in heavy brush at the base of a big hill. Second, despite Calvin's most convincing rattling, the buck would not leave his newfound girlfriends. Third, Gregg and Calvin were hiding atop the hill, about 200 yards away, and there was no way to sneak closer. Each time Calvin rattled, the buck charged to the edge of the heavy cover, but it would not come up the hill.

Gregg used a laser rangefinder to determine the distance and then asked Calvin to rattle one more time. Securely resting the new .50-caliber T/C Encore, Gregg mulled his "drops" and made a well-educated estimate on where to hold the scope's

Gun shops and mail-order catalogs offer a wide assortment of projectiles for muzzleloading deer hunters. Commercial muzzleloading bullets fall into four categories: saboted, round-balls, lead conicals and specialized bullet designs.

cross-hairs. The shot would be 190 yards, on a slight angle downward. After Calvin rattled, the big buck was suddenly at the familiar stopping point, hackles up and challenging, but not about to leave the does. Gregg fired and the buck was dead before it hit the ground. Calvin let out a whoop and vowed that he had never seen a buck die so quickly. That's significant, because Calvin has watched many bucks hit the dust.

One well-placed 250-grain PTX bullet, propelled by three 50-grain Pyrodex Pellets, killed the buck instantly. Gregg was confident he could place the bullet because he had practiced out to 200 yards. At that range, the Encore in-line was grouping inside a 4-inch circle consistently.

Not everyone shoots as much as Gregg, nor do they have the skill and knowledge to make 200-yard shots.

But this story shows the potential that most new in-line muzzleloaders possess. Such accuracy requires combining superb bullets, high-quality optics, uniform propellants and state-of-the-art manufacturing procedures. All that, plus a shooter who knows what he is doing, makes for effective deer hunting.

Bullets and Sabots for Whitetails

On that hunt, Gregg was also testing T/C's then-new PTX bullet, and it obviously performed perfectly, striking where he aimed and mushrooming with devastating effect. Today's muzzleloading shooters have never had such a variety of bullets for their in-line rifles.

Only a few years ago, the choice was patched round-balls or heavily lubed conicals. Many shooters had to cast their own projectiles because there weren't many

Manufacturers color-code sabots to indicate bore size and correct bullet fit. The sabot's petal thickness is increased or decreased to make up for diameter fluctuations in bullet diameters.

choices in the gun shops. That's a tremendous contrast to the sabot shooters who dominate most ranges today. Shooting a muzzleloader has never been more simple, reliable and accurate.

Gun shops and mail-order catalogs offer a wide assortment of bullets, round-balls, powders and sabots. Speaking of sabots, most shooters aren't sure how to pronounce this French-sounding word. "SAY-bo" works well, as does "Su-BOW," or just blain "sabutt." Regardless of how the word is pronounced, the little plastic sleeves helped revolutionize muzzleloader shooting. Virtually every manufacturer of bullets and muzzleloading rifles offers a line of saboted bullets.

Let's get something straight: most sabot sizes are what you think they are. Sabots in .45-, .50- and .54-caliber are the size of the bore. Unfortunately, bullet sizes are not always what we assume. Most muzzleloading bullets put into sabots were originally intended for handgun use. But .38s are really

.357, .44s are actually .429 and .45s can be .451 for pistols or .458 for rifles, as in .45-70. Because a bullet is, in effect, being shimmed by the sabot to fit the bore size, different thicknesses of the sabot's petals or sides must be used to ensure correct bore fit.

Manufacturers have color-coded their sabots to indicate bore size and correct bullet fit. The popular .50-caliber muzzleloader requires a different sabot if the shooter selects a .44 bullet (remember, it's actually .429) or a .45-caliber bullet. The green sabots properly hold a .44 bullet, because the petals are thicker and make up for the narrower bullet diameter. Black sabots have thinner petals and fit only .45, or .451, bullets.

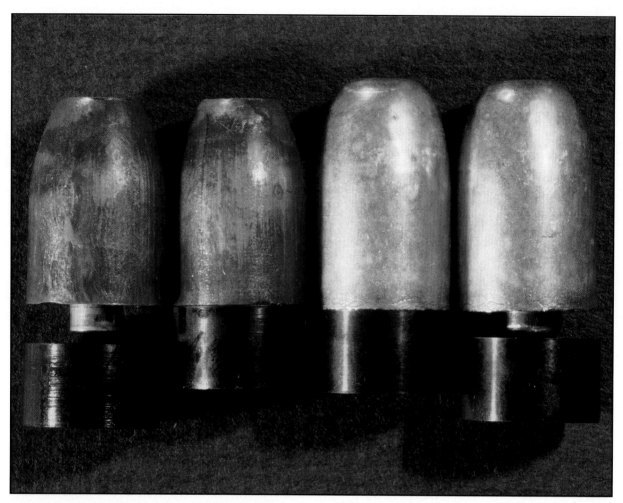

The Black Belt bullet from Big Bore Express features a plastic cup that is sized .001-inch larger than the bullet's diameter. Upon ignition, the cup — called a power check — seals the gases and presses into the rifling. This tight seal guides the bullet down the bore with speed, power and accuracy. Upon leaving the muzzle, the cup falls away, and the bullet drives toward the target.

Varying Petal Lengths and Custom Jobs

To further complicate this situation, sabots can have varying petal lengths to fit long or short bullets. I've used at least three different .50-caliber black sabots, all with different petal lengths. Obviously, sabots must fit correctly or else accuracy suffers drastically. In one recent experiment, I purposely tried a short bullet in a long sabot. Not surprisingly, the velocity dropped and the accuracy was terrible.

Just to keep everyone on their toes, manufacturers also designed .50-caliber high pressure sabots, which will withstand the higher velocities generated by shooting three 50-grain Pyrodex Pellets. These sabots are orange and have two petal lengths. The latest sabot design uses a stepped base design that further strengthens the sabot for shooting hot loads.

Thompson/Center also makes an excellent sabot called the Break-o-Way. This three-piece assembly uses two plastic sleeves held together by a lubricated wool base ring or "doughnut." This design results in quick separation of the sabot from the bullet. Accuracy is very good with T/C's lead HP or XTP bullets. Break-o-Way sabots are available separately for use with any .44-caliber (.429- to .430-inch) bullet.

White and Gonic developed saboted bullets for their unique-diameter barrels. These companies occasionally used different colors and shapes for their sabots to indicate the difference in size and fit.

Big Bore Express in Idaho developed the Black Belt, an innovative bullet design that combines features of a conical and saboted bullet. BBE took the bottom of an MMP sabot

DEEP PENETRATION Hardened lead tough enough for deep terminal penetration on tough-skinned game.

minus the petals, and attached this plastic cup to a bullet that is .001 inch undersized. The result is a bullet that seats smoothly and securely, as the "power check" (hollow plastic base) maintains an even fit in the barrel. Upon ignition, the hollow base seals the gases, and the detonation causes the bullet to swell slightly into the rifling, causing the projectile to spin. The power check separates from the bullet after leaving the barrel, similar to sabots. These bullets are the easiest-seating bullets on the market, and they stay in place and shoot very accurately. The latest Black Belts have a copper-coating that is electroplated onto a lead core, and they're marketed by CVA.

Bullet Categories

Commercial muzzleloading bullets can be placed into four categories: round-balls, lead conicals, saboted (lead or jacketed), and custom-design such as the Black Belt.

Round-balls are probably the earliest projectiles fired from black-powder rifles,

Round-balls are probably the earliest muzzleloading projectiles and are still widely used by traditional muzzleloading enthusiasts. Even so, the author has concerns about their aerodynamics and penetrating ability for whitetail hunting.

and they're still used by many primitive-weapons aficionados. I have concerns about the round-ball's penetrating ability, even though countless thousands of whitetails have been killed with them during North America's history. Round-balls do not have much mass and they're not aerodynamic. I have also heard of round-balls flattening out, turning on edge, taking the path of least resistance, and slitting a small exit hole in the hide. Round-balls simply can't break bones as effortlessly and penetrate as deeply as conical bullets. Although some round-ball shooters prefer to cut their own patches, most shooters use round commercial patches of the proper size and material.

Conical muzzleloading bullets still have a

Buffalo Bullet Co. is North America's largest manufacturer of conical bullets.

following with many hunters, particularly those who want maximum penetration for hunting larger animals. Maxi-style bullets are usually accurate in a wide variety of barrels and twist rates. Conicals range in weight from around 240 grains in .45-caliber slugs to 560 grains in the .58-caliber bore. Most conicals are fairly tight-fitting to start, but after being "engraved" by the rifling, they go smoothly down the bore.

Bullet Manufacturers

Buffalo Bullet Co. from Santa Fe Springs, Calif., is the largest manufacturer of conical bullets. In 1981, this company was the first to manufacture pre-lubricated bullets. Buffalo Bullets have a reputation for accuracy on the range and consistent performance on big game. These cold-formed hollow-point bullets are offered in calibers from .36 to .58.

T/C's Maxi-Ball and the newer Maxi-Hunter are a pair of proven performers on big game. Both shoot well in various rifles tested, and they retain most of their initial weight, regardless of how much bone and tissue they break or penetrate. T/C sells its maxi-bullets in sturdy plastic boxes of 20, or in handy Pocket Packs of two plastic tubes with five bullets each.

Hornady also sells conical muzzleloading bullets. Its Great Plains bullets perform nicely on deer-sized critters as well as bigger game.

A relative newcomer to the bullet scene is PB Custom from Winnipeg, Manitoba. PB Custom makes a wide variety of standard-bore bullets, as well as some great shooting slugs for the Gonic rifle.

Any discussion of saboted, jacketed bullets should probably begin with the widely used Hornady XTP. The XTP is produced in .357, .44 and .45 calibers. The .44- and .45-caliber bullet weights range from 185 to 300 grains. Hornady supplies XTPs to several major

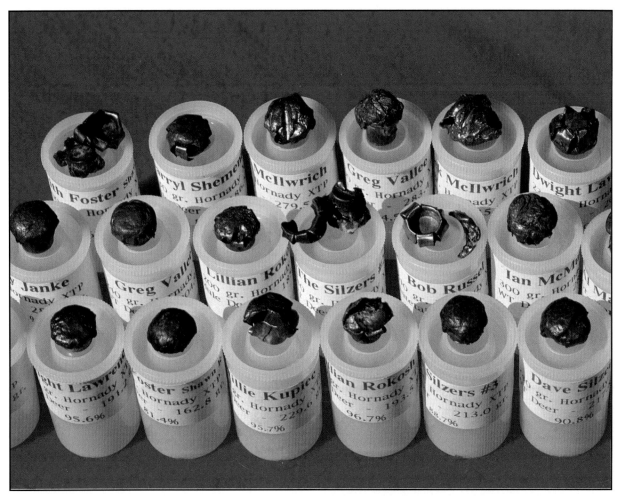

The recovered bullets above are Hornady XTP bullets. The author has found their performance on big game consistent and reliable.

players in the muzzleloading field, including T/C. The basic XTP design has been improved to ensure the bullets stand up to muzzleloading velocities. I have 15 XTPs in my collection of recovered bullets. Their performance on big game is consistent and reliable, particularly the .45-caliber slugs weighing 300 grains.

The Barnes X-Bullet for muzzleloading is pure copper and has attracted a significant following of serious hunters. The Barnes engineers have delivered a bullet that achieves very uniform expansion at a wide variety of velocities. This is true of both 250- and 300-grain bullets for .50-caliber rifles, as well as the 325-grain version for .54-caliber barrels. My recovered X-Bullets are mostly 300-grain units taken from moose and elk, but I also have a couple of the 250-grain slugs that performed beautifully on deer. These recovered bullets had not lost any weight, period. The petals all curled back perfectly. Barnes X-Bullets are marketed by some of the major muzzleloading companies

under a variety of brand names.

Modern Muzzleloading also markets lead and jacketed saboted bullets for its .50- and .54-caliber Knight Rifles. The Knight Rifle folks recommend the 240- or 260-grain jacketed bullets for deer, and the 300- or 325-grain slugs for moose, elk and big bears. Knight also markets 260- and 310-grain lead hollow-points, and I would be hard-pressed to recommend one over the other for whitetails. My son and I have shot a lot of these bullets, particularly the 310-grain lead hollow-point in our .50-caliber guns. They are the most uniformly accurate bullet we use. The 310s we have recovered from game have averaged 94 percent weight-retention. These are fine hunting bullets.

The Buffalo Bullets company designed its saboted lead bullets with hollow points and boattail bases. Available in .45-, .50- and .54-

The Barnes X-Bullet is solid copper and designed for controlled expansion. This bullet is also marketed by other muzzleloading companies under various names.

caliber bores, these bullets are typical of the precision expected from Buffalo. Its .50- and .54-caliber bullets share the same 225-, 252- and 302-grain dimensions, but come with appropriate sabots.

Buffalo Bullets also offers a copper-plated 240-grain bullet called the T.C.P. (Totally Copper Plated), which is a superb hunting slug. This bullet is basically a pure lead conical with a thin coating of copper plating similar to copper-coated rimfire bullets. Expansion is guaranteed, because there is no jacket that might be too thick to allow mushrooming. The TCPs are sold in boxes of 50 with sabots for .50- or .54-caliber bores.

Several other bullet manufacturers, including Nosler, Speer and Sierra sell .44- and .45-caliber pistol bullets that are suitable for muzzleloading or designed specifically for muzzleloading. Federal also markets its popular Trophy Bonded muzzleloading

bullets, which have proven extremely reliable for deer and other game.

Remington's bullets include round-balls, conicals and jacketed bullets in sabots. The round-balls are unique because they feature a golden coating. Remington's Copper Solid sabot shotgun slugs have been very successful, so the company adapted the technology to develop a 289-grain muzzleloading bullet. I have used Remington's 303-grain jacketed bullet with excellent results on the range. I also have one recovered 303-grainer that a friend's 12-year-old daughter used on her first deer. Ashley Miller shot the muley buck at 90 yards after sneaking up on several bedded animals. The bullet traveled diagonally initially, then appeared to bounce off the inside rib cage, which took it through the lungs before stopping inside the front shoulder on the entrance side. The mushroom was perfect, and the spent slug weighs still 302.6 grains!

Swift Bullets, makers of the famous A-Frame, have a line of muzzleloader bullets that retain 100 percent of their initial weight virtually every time. These beautifully

finished .44- and .45-caliber bullets are so shiny that they're almost too nice to shoot! Swift markets these bullets in boxes of 50 or in handy blister-packs complete with .50- or .54-caliber sabots. Swift A-Frame bullets are also marketed by Knight Rifles in weights ranging from 220 grains to 325 grains. I have used these bullets on several hunts with excellent success.

A Look at Recovered Bullets

I'm trying to find out which bullets work best on game, because I don't believe shooting holes in paper has any relevance in predicting a bullet's effectiveness on living tissue.

As a result, for several years I've been collecting recovered slugs from big-game kills, both by me and those made by friends and associates. By early 2000, my collection had grown to more than 75 bullets, including a wide assortment of brands and styles recovered from six species of big game. My network of hunters continues to provide bullets and information after each hunting season. I have data sheets and measuring

These bullets are Nosler Partitions. The bullet's lead tip expands while the jacketed lead core remains intact. This design makes for a deep-penetrating bullet.

criteria for every bullet in the collection. Shooting distances range from 10 yards to more than 200 yards, and my data include the animal's body position, reaction, internal damage. I also record several measurements of changes to the shape of each bullet.

I've found I need at least five bullets before considering any conclusions, and at least 15 bullets before confirming a trend. Statisticians might scoff at those numbers, but a lineup of 15 bullets of the same make and manufacturer shows me what to expect. Even five bullets is likely to indicate how well a bullet model retains weight and reacts to impacts with bones and tissue.

One of the recovered Hornady XTP bullets actually fell onto the serving platter as a venison roast was being sliced! This whitetail had been standing head-on, and the slug entered the right front shoulder and stopped in the left hip. There was so little tissue damage that the butcher hadn't notice the

Remington Core-Lokt bullets are designed to retain nearly 100 percent of their weight upon expansion. The author recovered the slug on the right from a mule deer shot by 12-year-old Ashley Miller in Saskatchewan.

wound channel as he cut and wrapped the roast. This is common bullet performance in muzzleloaders, as the bullets shed velocity and energy within the deer. Typically, there is not the hemorrhaging and destruction around the entrance and exit wounds that is characteristic of centerfire rifle bullets. Muzzleloading bullets penetrate deeply, and have the energy to break bones, but they usually don't inflict extreme shock and tissue damage.

We have been taught that the classic mushroom shape indicates optimum bullet performance. Mushroomed bullets look great, but do they kill any better than bullets that keep their original shape or took on some other form? Mushrooming no doubt enhances the transfer of energy to the animal because the bullet's frontal area enlarges. And this shape

might help break bones, depending on retained velocity, but mushroomed bullets always penetrate less than non-mushroomed bullets because of their large frontal surface. The larger their front surface, the more resistant they are to penetration.

Our group has recovered a few bullets that failed to expand or open up much, yet they killed the animal as quickly as the most classic "mushrooms" in my collection. This leads me to an important conclusion: Whether the projectile is lead, jacketed, round-ball, hollow point, saboted or whatever, bullet placement is the most important factor in making clean kills.

Terminal performance varies significantly with bullet design. Pure lead bullets that upset quickly shed energy much more rapidly than controlled-expansion bullets. Many hunters don't realize the bullet's size and frontal area greatly influence how deeply it penetrates. Many slower bullets out-penetrate faster ones because they have a smaller frontal area and don't shed energy

Down-Range Velocities

(In Feet Per Second)

Bullet	Muzzle	100 yards	200 Yards
180 RedHot	2,194	1,754	1,359
200 RedHot	2,198	1,689	1,422
220 RedHot	2,083	1,669	1,413
250 RedHot	2,045	1,626	1,320
300 RedHot	1,923	1,545	1,312

Figure 9-1. The author measured the muzzle and down-range velocity of various RedHot bullet weights. Each of the RedHot bullets (the same as the Barnes X-Bullet) in the chart was shot from a Knight DISC rifle using a 150-grain charge of Pyrodex Pellets. The muzzle and 100-yard figures represent a 10-shot average, and the 200-yard figure is a five-shot average.

as quickly.

The following chart shows some down-range velocities of a relatively hot load with a selection of Barnes muzzleloading X-Bullets, which are sold as RedHot bullets by Knight Rifles (see Figure 9-1). As you can see, some lighter bullets lose velocity much faster than heavier models after 100 yards.

The terminal performance of most muzzleloading bullets today is remarkably uniform over a wide range of impact velocities. I have many examples of recovered bullets that were shot at fairly long range. These bullets all mushroomed nicely and penetrated deeply. However, they typically don't mushroom as fully as on close-range shots. In addition, the bullets don't appear to have tumbled, because there is rarely damage on the base or heal.

A Case Example

My buddy Chopper shot a huge cow moose at point-blank range with a popular 300-grain, .50-caliber bullet. A few minutes after I heard the shot, I walked over and found him standing speechless. He was wide-eyed and slapping his chest as if to keep his heart pounding. I asked what he had shot at, but he couldn't answer. He mumbled about his heart, and how he hadn't been so excited since his first "sexual experience." Finally he quit shaking and started to speak coherently. He claimed he had shot in self-defense when a cow moose almost trotted over him!

He had been sitting on the ground, listening to my moose-calling attempts, when the cow ran down a trail straight at him. Chopper swore he was aiming nearly straight up when he shot. In reality, the shot was almost 15 yards long, which was close enough from Chopper's viewpoint. After the shot, the moose whirled into the heavy bush and died within 20 paces. The bullet had hit the cow square in the brisket, penetrating all the way to her rumen. We found the bullet in perfect shape. Even though no mushrooming occurred, the moose was dead in seconds.

I don't advocate hard-point bullets, but I think muzzleloading bullets can efficiently kill deer as long as they strike vital areas. Shot placement is the key to clean kills. We've killed many whitetails that literally dropped in their tracks. Shot placement is the main reason, but another important factor is shooting distance. We're usually so close we're certain to hit the vitals. Aiming a shot to break the spine or destroy the nervous system is possible at close range.

Chest-hit whitetails run for a distance, but because most muzzleloading bullets exit, there is usually a good blood trail. Because of their large bore size, muzzleloading bullets make large entrance and exit holes, usually allowing good blood flow.

Do mushrooming bullets kill deer more cleanly and efficiently? Yes and no. Bullets that mushroom transfer more energy to the animal, but the resulting mushroom shape decreases penetration.

A few notes to help you figure out where your shot hit: Chest-hit deer usually run hard in the direction they're pointing. Heart-shot deer usually run as if their front legs are shorter than their rear, on a slight forward angle. Gut-shot deer instantly hump-up and then make a wild dash. The most gratifying result is something we call the "Bang-Flop," which occurs when a bullet simply overwhelms the deer's nervous system and drops it on the spot.

Black-Powder Loads for Whitetails

Muzzleloaders are devastating on whitetails, but shooters must do their part. If close-range shooting is your objective, and you don't intend to shoot past 50 or 75 yards, fairly light loads will work well. I would say that 70 grains of powder is a reasonable minimum for short-range deer hunting. This load will produce muzzle velocities of at least 1,300 or 1,400 feet per second, depending on the bullet weight. The current maximum charges of 150 grains, either with powder or Pyrodex Pellets, produce much faster velocities in the 2,000 fps range with 250-grain bullets. Of course, these high-end loads also generate more recoil, smoke and noise.

Despite the above, I still recommend bullet weights no lighter than 200 grains, with the optimum weight being 250 grains. Because each rifle has its own temperament, you must do some test shooting to find the best bullet-and-powder combinations. Once you find the load that works consistently for your rifle, stay with it. Confidence in your equipment and hunting skills is extremely important in killing that big buck.

CHAPTER 10

How Far Should You Shoot?

Most of us can wring much more performance from our in-line rifles, but there is a price. We must put time and effort into shooting at the range to confidently extend our effective range. How far dare we go? That is determined first by your ability and then by each projectile's relatively poor ballistics efficiency.

How far will an in-line muzzleloading rifle shoot accurately? Unfortunately, there is no definitive answer. So many variables affect accuracy that no one can say an individual model of in-lines will reliably shoot "x-hundred" yards. Besides the limitations of the systems used for propelling a projectile, the primary variable is shooting skill.

Because modern in-line rifles frequently look like centerfire rifles, many people assume the newer models offer significantly more performance than older muzzleloaders. In fact, when comparing the accuracy of in-line muzzleloaders with the accuracy of sidehammers, there isn't any difference. When firing identical loads in both styles of black-powder rifles with similar barrel lengths, Thompson/Center's chronograph tests revealed absolutely no difference in velocities. That makes sense because black powder can only release a given amount of energy, and manufacturers have ensured that black-powder substitutes release energy similar in power to those generated by the original black powder.

Many shooters dispute this fact, saying, "The new in-lines are faster and shoot farther; the advertising says so!" But one cannot compare an in-line that's shooting light saboted bullets propelled by three Pyrodex Pellets with a sidehammer shooting a big conical pushed by 90 grains of FFG black powder. Until recent years, lightweight saboted bullets were strictly the domain of in-line shooters, while side-

The whitetail's vital zone is roughly a circular area that encompasses the heart area (red), lung region (pink), and shoulder/spine region (yellow). These vitals create the optimum target for most hunters.

hammer shooters tried to maximize the performance of the patched round-ball or a big, heavy conical. That world is changing, however, as manufacturers put identical barrels on each style of muzzleloading rifle. Shooting lightweight bullets accurately at high speed is primarily a factor of barrel twist, powder charge and barrel length. Some companies have designed traditional muzzleloaders to use the latest technology, and the performance of these rifles exactly matches the hottest-shooting in-lines.

We have always accepted that muzzleloaders are short-range firearms, and most hunters believe a primary objective of black-powder hunting is to get as close as possible to the deer before shooting. Most shooters sight in their in-lines at 100 yards and plan to shoot out to that distance. The fact is, scoped in-lines

or sidehammers are accurate and lethal at significantly farther ranges than 100 yards.

Most of us can wring much more performance from our in-line rifles, but there is a price. We must put time and effort into shooting at the range to confidently extend our effective range. How far dare we go? That is determined first by your ability and then by the projectile's relatively poor ballistics. For expert marksmen, this order is reversed. In other words, some shooters have the skill to capably shoot a rifle farther than what their in-line can accurately reach.

But muzzleloading rifles have a maximum range that varies significantly with the load and the shooter. Most in-line rifles will group three shots into 2- to 3-inch groups at 100 yards. In a perfect world, that should translate into 4- to 6-inch groups at 200 yards and 6- to 9-inch groups at 300 yards. In the real world, with wind blowing, heart pounding and shots taken from atop shooting sticks instead of a benchrest, the group sizes will no doubt be larger.

The Whitetail's Vital Zone

Next, compare that assumption with realistic accuracy requirements for hunting whitetails. The whitetail's vital zone encompasses the heart, lungs and the chest area, including the forward portion of the spine. This vital zone is basically everything ahead of the deer's diaphragm, and it makes for the optimum target for most hunters. The vital zone, of course, varies in actual size with the deer, with Deep South whitetails being considerably smaller in body than Northern whitetails. In addition, bucks are usually larger than does.

In effect, a white-tailed buck's vital zone can be described as a volley-ball lying between and slightly behind of the front shoulders. That makes for a 12- to 15-inch roughly circular area. That means a whitetail's vital zone is a fairly large target. Put another way, we might say a "minute of whitetail" is 12 to 15 minutes of angle at 100 yards. A 12- to 15-inch vital zone equates to 6 to 7½ MOA at 200 yards, and 4 to 5 MOA at 300 yards. This still represents fairly reasonable shooting requirement.

On the bench, many muzzleloading hunters can shoot 2- to 4-inch groups at 100 yards, 4- to 6-inch groups at 200 yards, and 6- to 9-inch groups at 300. But in hunting situations, wind, excitement and the absence of a solid rest often diminish accuracy.

Before you decide I'm full of bull-droppings, try shooting your scoped in-line in 50-yard increments out past 100 yards. Be sure to use a target that's large enough to catch the drop, because muzzleloading trajectories are steep after 100 yards. You'll probably be amazed at the accuracy you can achieve. What follows are the results from one of my many tests out to 300 yards with a couple of accurate in-line muzzleloaders. Both rifles carry high-quality scopes. The Knight was equipped with a 3-9X Nikon Monarch and the T/C a Simmons Aetec 2.5-8X model.

This particular test might have produced exceptional results, because I have done a huge amount of shooting. The rifles performed uniformly, and produced similar groups when I

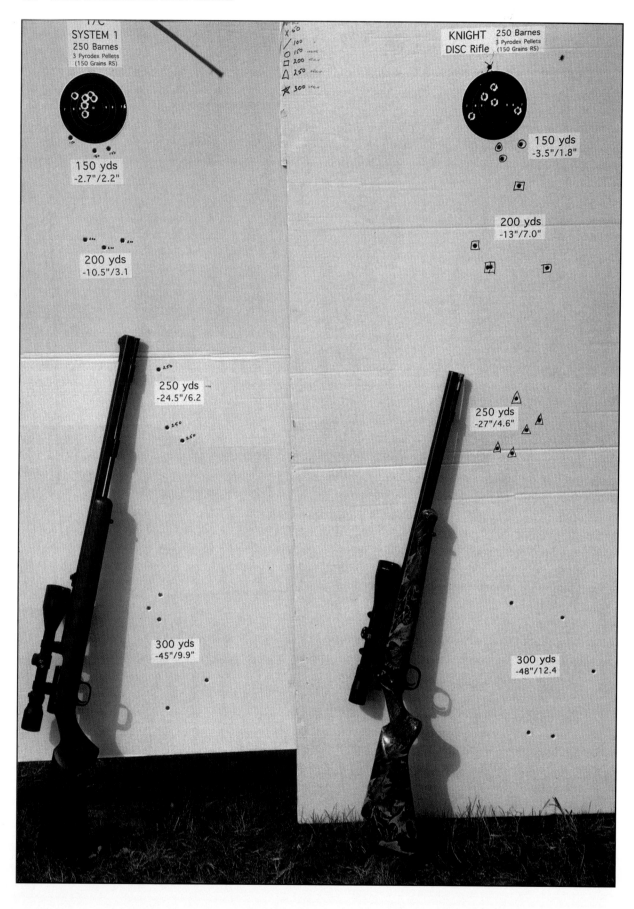

300-Yard Drop Test

Yardage:	100	150	200	250	300

Drop in Inches

	100	150	200	250	300
Knight DISC	0	-3.3	-12	-26	-47
T/C System 1	0	-2.7	-10.8	-24.8	-45

Accuracy (Group Size)

	100	150	200	250	300
Knight DISC	1.3	2.2	4	5.2	8.1
T/C System 1	1.5	2.1	3.3	6.2	7.7

Figure 10-1. The author tested bullet drop by shooting the Knight DISC rifle and the Thompson/Center System 1 out to 300 yards. He used a high-pressure load consisting of saboted 250-grain Barnes X-Bullets and 150 grains of Pyrodex Pellets in both rifles. The results shown are the averages from three 3-shot groups.

asked two other marksmen to repeat this 300-yard test. I'm the first to agree that 300 yards is a long shot for an in-line muzzleloader, but some shooters and rifles are capable of exceptional accuracy at that distance.

Wind becomes a significant factor during such shooting. Shooting in wind is a skill that can be sharpened by practicing and carefully noting wind drift under various conditions. The fact is, long-range shooting requires time and effort on the range, which is much more than some hunters are willing to expend.

The retained energy of these loads is still lethal at long range, despite what some computer-generated tables indicate. External ballistics are decided by muzzle velocity and the bullet's aerodynamic shape, or lack thereof. Without getting too technical, let's say some styles of 250-grain saboted bullets will pass through a white-tailed buck at 200 yards, and I have seen shots pass through at ranges considerably farther.

I also have a bullet recovered from a large moose that passed through the chest and stopped under the far hide on a 200-yard shot.

Setting up for Long-Range Shooting

Allow me to explain how I prepared for a "just-in-case" scenario where a long shot is required. A while back, I was invited to hunt Nilgai antelope in South Texas with Tony Knight of Modern Muzzleloading. We were warned that some of the shooting possibilities might be long for muzzleloaders. I decided to mount a Burris Signature 3-9X scope onto a super-shooting Knight Big Horn in-line rifle. This particular Burris scope has target turrets and a mildot reticle. Mildots were developed to enable accurate range estimation for military snipers, and they have great application for hunting. The mildot reticle provides constant reference points on the cross-hairs, so hold-offs can be made with excellent "repeatability."

First, I determined that the Big Horn shot most accurately with a charge of two Pyrodex Pellets and the 325-grain Swift A-Frames that I wished to field-test on a Nilgai. Many of the three-shot groups I test-fired stayed inside 1½ inches at 100 yards if I did my part. After I was comfortable with this load's accuracy, I proceeded to shoot in 50-yard intervals out to the 300-yard maximum available at our local rifle range. I set my point of impact at 100 yards exactly at zero, instead of the 3-inch high setting preferred by hunters.

I also set up 7-foot high sheets of cardboard to ensure each shot hit paper, regardless of how far it dropped. My shooting tests indicated the 325-grain Swift A-Frames dropped 12 inches at 200 yards and 57 inches at 300 yards. I marked a large "X" at the center of each group and returned to the bench. After realign-

No long-distance shot should be attempted without precisely determining the actual distance. A laser rangefinder should be carried in a handy pocket and used to measure the deer's actual distance or the distance of nearby landmarks.

ing the scope on the original aiming mark, the large X's allowed me to clearly see the centers of the 200- and 300-yard groups. I zoomed the scope magnification, changing the field of view until one mildot — which happened to be the second dot from the cross-hair intersection — moved exactly to the 300-yard point of impact. At 4.5X, the top of the second mildot became my 300-yard zero. I shot several groups at 300 yards by aiming with the top of the mildot, and was pleased to shoot a group in the 7- to 8½-inch range. At 200 yards, using the top of the first mildot, I shot a group that was 2 inches high. My Big Horn rifle shot excellent 200-yard groups, with a couple of three-shot groups just barely exceeding the 3-inch mark. At 100 yards, I simply used the cross-hair intersection. I estimated shots in

between the 100-yard increments by holding between each appropriate mildot.

I practiced these holds until I was confident in my shooting abilities at these extreme ranges. As long as I didn't move the scope's power ring, I maintained my zeros. Therefore, I knew if I had to shoot at such long distances, I would not have to estimate how much to hold over.

Pinpointing the Bullet's Impact

One might assume we've taken care of the long-range shooting challenges, but that was only the beginning. Two major factors must be known before attempting any long shot. First, you must know precisely the actual shooting distance. Second, you must know what effect wind will have on the bullet.

Pinpointing actual distances has become much easier with the advent of laser rangefinders. Bushnell lasers quickly became a standard hunting tool in my muzzleloading kit, because they're small and easy to carry. They have become almost as important as good

binoculars to our deer hunting.

Although we occasionally have time to "laser" a distance off a deer while hunting, that's not something you can anticipate or expect. It's far better to use the laser when first stopping or sitting at a particular site to gather key distances to objects where you might spot a deer.

Shooting in wind is not so easily mastered as rangefinding, but it's not as difficult as many hunters assume. The main factors to consider are the distance to the target, the bullet's speed and its shape, and the wind's speed and direction. Although practice and experience are great assets, you don't have to go it alone in learning to "dope" the wind. Relatively simple charts can help determine where to hold to compensate for wind. I carry a great little wind-meter made by Minox, so I have quick information available to compare with notes I've taken to help figure hold-offs.

Even with all the information and practice, however, there will still be instances when you should pass up a shot. If you're not confident

Muzzleloading bullets strike deer at lower velocities and don't create the enormous shock and hydrostatic effects of centerfire bullets. As a result, shot placement is more critical for quick kills when hunting with an in-line muzzleloading rifle.

in your ability to adjust for wind-drift, turn down the shot and make a commitment to put more time in on the range.

A Few Thoughts on Ethics

Many hunters have strong opinions on the ethics of taking long shots at deer, whether with a muzzleloader or a flat-shooting center-fire rifle. I think no hunter has a right to impose his ethics on someone else. Ethics are based on personal skills, individual decisions, respect for the deer, and the love of hunting. Every hunter's ethics should be within boundaries set by our society's laws and regulations. Anything short of that tags you as a poacher and violator. Anything above that gives you a lot of latitude to enjoy deer hunting.

The most important moments of a hunt are the seconds that tick away before we squeeze the trigger. This is the moment we must do our part as hunters. Shooting ability is all important and, with muzzleloaders, there's seldom a chance for a follow-up shot. Shoot straight the first time, as did the hunter at right, and you'll have good reason to be proud.

Whether we're discussing long shots, running shots, or shots in thick cover that offer only a tiny view of the vitals, we must realize that the standards are as varied as individual shooting skills.

Any hunter can suggest techniques and attitudes that might offer more enjoyment or challenge. Those are some of the joys of the sport. I despise the arrogance of those who assume they're better, more ethical hunters. If my friend can kill deer cleanly and consistently at 250 yards with an open-sighted muzzleloader, I won't condemn him just because my shooting skills aren't as sharp. After all, even thought most hunters aren't Olympic shooters, we shouldn't assume everyone is just an average shooter. Unfortunately, many hunters who have strong feelings on long shots are too lazy to learn how to extend their effective range. It's much more convenient to condemn others from behind a facade of misguided ethics.

The most important moments of a hunt are the seconds that tick away as we aim a rifle, position the sights or cross-hair, and squeeze the trigger. These are the moments we're about to take a life, and they're filled with jumpy nerves, shortness of breath and high expectations. This is the moment we must do our part as hunters. Shooting ability becomes all-important. We cannot recall a bullet, and with muzzleloading, there is seldom a chance for a make-up shot.

After having said all of this, I much prefer short-range shots than long shots. Because I have been a fanatical shooter for decades, I can place the bullet exactly. When I shoot, I'm confident the deer will die instantly if I do my part. There is usually more challenge to getting close, and this is accompanied by lots of excitement. But, if the deer is 200 yards away,

Trigger control, breathing, cheek-weld, and other target shooting factors are always significant, no matter the distance. Many hunters take these basics for granted as they prepare for and take a shot. The fact is, these basics of accurate shooting are as important in the field as they are on the range.

Flinching is one of the most common causes of inaccurate shooting. Shooters who jerk the trigger in anticipation of recoil cannot control their sight picture. Flinching also causes missed deer or worse, wounding. This is another important reason for practice on the range. If you don't practice frequently, it's difficult to overcome flinching. After all, flinching is simply mind over matter, and it can only be stopped with adequate concentration and determination.

Tony Knight offers two methods that usually beat the flinching habit. First, the shooter should have someone else be responsible for capping the in-line, or controlling the secondary safety. If the shooter never knows if the rifle has been capped or "double-safed," he will quickly learn the severity of his flinch. Knight also recommends shooting with both eyes open to minimize the tendency to close the shooting eye during a flinch.

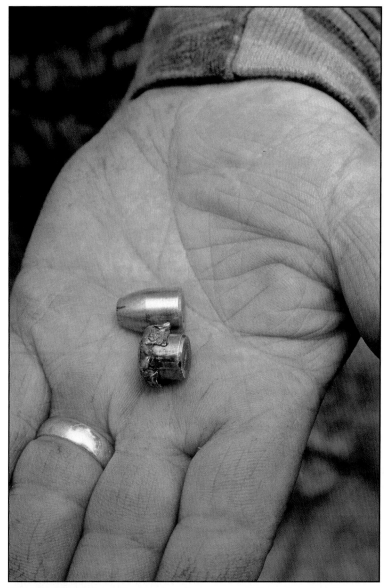

When hunting, the author prefers short-range shots rather than long shots. However, years of target practice have made him proficient at long-range shots, when a good shooting rest is available and time allows its use. At left, the author poses with a Nilgai antelope he shot at more than 300 yards in South Texas. The recovered bullet, above, displays the excellent expansion characteristic of good velocity.

Fun Shooting for In-Line Practice

Although we've been primarily discussing long-range shooting, any shooting is better than no shooting when preparing for a hunt. My friends and I have several shooting games we enjoy with our in-lines at the range. The whole idea is to shoot, and the more fun you have, the more you'll shoot. Our fun-shoots combine luck and skill, with the emphasis on skill. What follows are some of our fun-shooting ideas.

1. Lath Cutting: Drive wooden surveyor's laths into the ground at ranges determined by the group, but usually at 50 yards. Shooting offhand, the first shooter to break off his lath wins.

2. Cutting 2-by-4s: Drive 3-foot 2x4s into the

the wind is not a factor, and my rifle is properly sighted for that range, I will shoot with confidence and expect a clean kill.

Practice and Flinch-Control

Shooting skills are developed and refined through training and practice. There is little difference between the mechanics of precise, close-range shooting at a small target and precise, long-range shooting at a large target.

ground. Groups of two or three shooters compete at 50 yards offhand to see which group can sever their board first, or cut it into three pieces! Increase or decrease the distance to make things interesting.

3. Egg Shooting: The competitor must hit an egg at 50 yards with a rest or 25 yards offhand.

4. Shooting Thumbtacks: The competitors take turns shooting offhand at a thumbtack at 15 to 25 yards. If you miss the tack, you're out. If you nick it, you shoot again. Your bullet must punch the tack clean through the backstop for a win.

5. Cutting Targets: From a rest, we shoot at standard targets cut into two pieces, vertically or horizontally, at 100 yards. The winner is determined by the best score. This is tougher than it sounds, because if your shot is even a half-inch off the bull's-eye your score is zero.

6. Call Your Score: The shooter calls the score of his next shot, but he keeps the score only if he makes the shot he calls. This offhand shooting game is best played with a large full-color archery target at 50 yards.

7. Shooting Crackers: Soda or Ritz crackers make great targets. Put up five per shooter at a tough distance. It's fun to watch them explode on impact. Let the birds clean up the mess!

8. 100 Grains: Each shooter gets exactly 100 grains of black powder or Pyrodex, and a fresh target at 15 paces. The shooter who puts the most shots into the paper wins. Tip: Some shooters measure powder with empty .22 long-rifle cases!

9. Clay Birds: Shooting standard clay targets at 45 to 50 yards offhand is very sporting. To separate the women from the girls, turn the clay targets on edge and face the shooters.

10. Cutting String: We have lots of variations on this one, including cutting individual strings, crossed strings (you have to cut both), and strings with hidden prizes dangling on them. We do this offhand, usually at about 20 yards.

Above are some items the author and his friends use to sharpen their marksmanship skills. Atop the board is an egg, and behind it on the stake is a balloon. Imaginative targets and shooting sessions make practice more entertaining than simply shooting at a paper bull's-eye.

All of these competitions can be made more interesting by placing small bets! Even at two bits per shot, these fun shoots prove interesting and competitive. Best of all, they improve your shooting skills by having fun while pulling the trigger.

CHAPTER 11

In-Line Deer Hunting and Tactics for Whitetails

Rifle-hunting tactics don't always work well during black-powder seasons. You must go back to the basics and learn how to hunt all over again. Or, if you're a bow-hunter, simply plan your in-line rifle hunts as if you were still using your bow and arrows. Scouting, more so than firepower, plays the major role.

"**M**uzzleloader hunting stinks! I can't hit a deer with this thing. The deer are always running or they're too far away! I'm always loading when I should be shooting!"

I've heard such words from many hunters after their first muzzleloading deer season, and I understand their frustration. Traditional rifle-hunting methods don't always work well during black-powder seasons. Unfortunately, many new muzzleloading hunters learn that the hard way. Muzzleloaders work best at close range, and they're not suited for untrained shots at running deer where follow-up firepower is crucial. Because

muzzleloading rifles offer only one chance, a major element of in-line hunting is making the most of each shot.

Fortunately, there's a simple answer to this frustration. Go back to the basics and learn how to hunt all over again. Or, if you're a bow-hunter, plan your in-line rifle hunts as if you were still using your bow and arrows. Successful muzzleloading deer hunters use many of the same techniques that work for archers. Scouting, more so than firepower, plays a major role in their hunting.

Learn as much as possible about deer movement, feeding patterns and seasonal habits. Scents, decoys,

Making the transition from a centerfire rifle to a muzzleloading rifle often requires a change in hunting tactics. However, bow-hunters will usually find the transition easier because they're accustomed to thinking in close-up terms.

camouflage, tree stands, rattling and calling, and thorough knowledge of whitetail behavior become essential for consistently killing deer. On top of that, you must make a conscientious effort to keeping your in-line rifle "battle-ready" at all times.

The Muzzleloader's Learning Curve

Because muzzleloading deer hunters must juggle myriad tasks, most go through a learning curve that takes several seasons to master. My friend Bob Russell is a good example. When Bob purchased his first in-line, he hunted hard for a couple of seasons without much success. In fact, he endured more frustration than anything, and was considering going back to his centerfire rifles for good. Bob and his friends conducted a lot of deer drives, and they tried to stalk feeding deer they spotted from a distance. Most of their shooting opportunities were at fleeing animals or at the outer range of their shooting ability.

One day Bob and I compared notes. I explained the hunting methods that worked for me, my son and our partners. We were regularly getting good numbers of deer, including some big bucks. Our methods were so different from Bob's that he became determined to try them the next deer season.

First, because camouflage clothing is legal for Saskatchewan's muzzleloading season, Bob began his new approach by outfitting himself and his two teenage sons in camo. He also traded in his old smokepoles for new Thompson/Center in-lines and fitted them with quality hunting scopes. Next, he bought scents, grunt tubes and rattling antlers for himself and his sons. Then they began refining their hunting loads and practicing with their new T/C rifles. More accessories followed, including speed-loaders and new binoculars. All of this was great fun, and Bob included his sons in the planning.

Bob has a great area to hunt less than 30 minutes from home. He and his boys began scouting the area about a month before opening day. By spending a lot of time glassing and watching, they figured out the deer's feeding routines and key travel lanes. The deer moved from bedding areas to feeding areas on well-used trails, and they often fed in the same spots

To increase your muzzleloading hunting success, learn as much as possible about deer movement, feeding patterns and seasonal habits. To that end, scouting plays a major role.

about the same time every evening. As the patterns became clear, Bob began planning how to ambush the deer as they moved to feed. He was especially interested in several good bucks in the herd.

As opening day approached, the excitement and anticipation mounted. Bob knew he and his sons would see deer and they figured the shots were going to be completely on their terms. Bob's ground-blind locations took the prevailing winds into consideration, and ensured the hunters could see the deer as they left cover. Most of the shots would be well under 100 yards, and possibly be as close as 25 yards if all went well.

All of the preparation paid off. Bob and his boys

Muzzleloading rifles work best at close range, and they're not suited for long, untrained shots, especially at running deer where follow-up firepower is crucial.

consistently got real close to deer, and they were having a ball. They did not fill their tags the first day, by any means, but they got some shots. Unfortunately, they missed. They also came to realize they needed to improve their "sitting-still" skills. They killed their first deer after a day or two, and with time filled all their tags. Bob shot a fine buck, but his greatest reward was the enjoyment of hunting with his sons. It just doesn't get any better than that.

Since that first year, Bob has continued to add to his bag of tricks. The next hunting accessories he tried were a couple of full-sized deer decoys. At first he borrowed my decoys and he quickly experienced how well they work. Flambeau decoys have provided Bob and the boys with many exciting experiences. In fact, several deer have made the fatal mistake of coming within inches of the plastic critters. After the 1999 season, Bob began planning to use tree stands during future hunts. Learning to use all these various "toys" became a big part of the deer hunt for the Russells.

Bob's muzzleloading evolution was typical of many hunters. In-line rifles are great hunting tools, but they impose limitations that must be recognized, understood and addressed. Hunting with an in-line is best likened to taking a step backward, and a chance to slow the pace and enjoy unique hunting challenges. I find that hunting with in-lines frequently consumes a person's hunting life. Several of my friends haven't hunted deer with their centerfires since getting into in-lines. I also see many archers pick up the in-line with great success. Archers usually understand the essential skills and accessories required to get close to deer, and they enjoy the extra hunting opportunity.

A Unique Flavor

Most muzzleloading hunts have a special flavor. Perhaps this relates to the "stepping back" aspect of having only one shot. Perhaps it also levels the playing field a bit, with everyone shooting a rifle of similar range and velocity. Despite the fervor in some sectors to up the ante with "2,000-plus feet per second" loads, the average deer hunter is well served with moderately heavy saboted bullets traveling at 1,600 or 1,700 fps.

The secret to muzzleloading success lies in accepting the limitations of the one-shot challenge, and making every effort to ensure this single shot is exactly placed. And, of course, consistently placing the perfect shot is best done at close range. The excitement and satisfaction of shooting a buck at 28 paces rather than 200 must be felt to be appreciated. Many hunters fail to realize that such shots can be obtained with skill, patience and knowledge.

Deer hunting with in-line rifles is no different than hunting with sidehammer percussion rifles. These two rifles share the same accessories, including cappers, ramrods, short-starters and speed-loaders. The difference is the presence of safeties, ease of mounting a scope, and scope-compatible stocks. Traditional black-powder hunters tend to carry their accessories in shoulder-slung possibles bags. In-line hunters are more likely to use a small fanny-pack, and to carry cappers and speed-loaders in designated pockets in their pants and jackets.

Each hunter has his own ideas on what to take into the field. One big variable is how much powder and how many caps and bullets to include. With the advent of improved speed-loader designs — and the various styles of cappers required for shotgun prim-

The excitement and satisfaction of taking the perfect shot at close range must be felt to be appreciated.

ers, musket caps and No. 11 percussion caps, hunters have many choices. The simplest hunting kit includes a capper, a few bullets loose in a pocket, and pre-measured powder charges inside 35 mm film canisters. From there we can go to self-contained tools that automatically load the powder and a bullet — saboted or conical — into the bore with one plunger stroke. While most hunters are comfortable carrying about five shots into the field, the number varies.

Blending In

Where legal, camo outfits can be a great asset for in-line hunters. Even so, I firmly believe that staying motionless and having the wind in your favor is more important than camo. Appropriate camo is worth wearing, but the colors, shades and hues should resemble the habitat colors for best effect. If you're going to wear camo, include gloves and a face mask. Naturally, the quieter the fabric, the better you'll be concealed. The new carbon activated scent-trapping suits are worth considering, but I'm not

Where legal during black-powder seasons, camouflage can be a great asset for in-line deer hunters. For best results, the fabric should be quiet, and its colors and pattern should resemble the habitat.

sure how you can hide the strong smells of cleaners and chemicals used to clean your in-line.

One item that often needs to be camouflaged is the rifle. I cannot understand why some hunters dress head to toe in camo and then carry a shining stainless steel tube into the woods. Camo stocks carrying stainless steel in-line barrels show the influence marketing experts have on hunters. We spray our in-lines with bow-paint, apply removable camo tape, or pull stretchy bow-socks over the barrels. This helps break up the outline and tone down the shine of stainless steel.

When hunting from a ground blind, use vegetation for the most effective camo. Finding a good "hide" in weeds, trees or tall grass overlooking a feeding area is an optimum setup for in-line hunting. We also use sheets of lightweight camo netting to supplement vegetation. In fact, we even wrap it around and over ourselves to break up the human outline and to keep out bugs. Try to find a spot with a big tree or post to lean against, because this helps break-up your outline.

In the forest, shooting lanes are a major consideration, particularly from ground blinds. Many of our setups border agricultural fields, so shooting lanes are not a problem. If you have a laser rangefinder, use it to pinpoint likely shooting distances as soon as you settle into the blind. I like to determine maximums, locating rocks or trees that pinpoint my personal maximum range of 200 yards. Then I check key trails and any other landmarks that might be useful if a deer appears near them. I also memorize my drops in 50-yard intervals, but

When still-hunting or hunting from a ground blind, use the surrounding vegetation to conceal your presence or to break up your outline. Lightweight camo netting can be used to supplement the effect.

some hunters write this information on a label and attach it to the rifle's side. A neat trick is to make a small label that fits inside the flip-up eyepiece cap of the Butler Creek lens protectors.

Setting Up for the Hunt

Once settled into the blind, take a few minutes to organize your reloading essentials. I keep my capper and speed-loader handy, and my short-starter front and center. If I'm in a ground blind, I often remove

the ramrod and keep it ready for use. I also find handy spots for my binoculars, laser rangefinder and whatever tote bag I'm carrying that day. Lastly, I set up my shooting sticks or bipod and make sure they're positioned to cover the most likely shooting angles. Shooting sticks are a wonderful hunting tool for in-lines. My son, Glen, and I have used Underwood shooting sticks for many years. Our sticks from Stoney Point also do a great job. Many of our buddies carry homemade crossed sticks that work fine. Some

Elevated stands are popular for deer hunting. However, access to reloading accessories and other items can be tricky if you're not prepared. The author suggests developing a system for keeping these items at your fingertips.

shooters, however, find bipods to be more handy. The Harris bipods or the super lightweight Snipepods are good options.

While discussing ground-blinds, I must also mention an effective method that is one step lower: pit blinds. Digging a pit so only your head sticks above ground sounds bizarre, but this is the only way you can hide effectively in some situations. Deer have a difficult time detecting a hunter in a strategically located pit blind. This tactic gives you a chance to go literally eye to eye with bucks. Of course, this idea isn't for everybody, because many hunters want more latitude to move around. But when all else fails, a well-placed pit can be a deadly way to get close to deer using major trails and feeding areas out of in-line shooting range. Of course, pits should only be dug after obtaining permission from the property owner. In addition, never leave a pit open, even overnight. If necessary, fill it back in after a hunting season.

We also take advantage of haystacks, large bales or old farm machinery for "natural" blinds. Anything deer are accustomed to that offers concealment will work. I know an individual who sat in an abandoned outhouse one evening after spotting a huge buck feeding in a clover field. The buck's favorite trail just

Today's in-line deer hunter will most likely forgo the traditional leather possibles bag for a modern-style hunting pack. The simplest hunting pack includes a (1) capper, (2) powder/pellet speedloader, (3) extra bullets, (4) Short starter and (5) extra ignition devices.

happened to pass near the outhouse on the edge of an abandoned homestead. Unfortunately, the "outhouse buck" failed to show that evening as my friend hunched in ambush. Even without a shot, it makes for a good story.

Tree stands, of course, offer great possibilities for in-line hunters, but always wear a safety belt or even better, a full-body harness, the entire time you're off the ground. Essentially, there are three or four distinct styles of tree stands available. Commercial models include self-climbers, hang-on stands, ladder stands and tripod stands. Many hunters build their own elevated stands, but I don't recommend this option unless you're an accomplished carpenter or welder. I've seen homemade stands that range from a couple of boards to elaborate shooting huts. Some of them, frankly, are death traps.

Elevated stands can be used almost everywhere in whitetail country. Their obvious advantage is increas-

After getting situated in a ground blind or tree stand, use a laser rangefinder to determine shooting distances of various objects, such as rocks and trees. Rangefinding the distance to active deer trails is also a good idea.

ing your ability to spot deer. Unfortunately, many elevated devices make it difficult to provide easy access to your reloading accessories. Be sure to bring along small screw-in hooks or belt-on straps with accessory hooks. With a little practice and experimentation, you can develop a system for keeping your rangefinder, binoculars, capper, ramrod and speed-loaders at your fingertips.

Late-Season Memories

Hunting in winter or winter-like conditions is another story. Although hunting when it's minus 30 degrees Fahrenheit is not everyone's idea of fun, cold weather is unavoidable. In fact, it's often conducive to excellent deer hunting in Northern states and Canada. Canadian outfitters have devised a variety of snug enclosures, usually with a heat source, for their deer hunters. These shelters range from plywood to camo-canvas, and their main purpose besides concealment is to keep a hunter warm enough to spend all day watching a scrape, trail or food source.

Scents, rattling, grunting and decoying provide many exciting hunting experiences for our group. One memorable hunt involved me; my friend Norm Fradet; his son Patrick, then 12 and making his first

Cold weather and deer hunting often go together in Northern states and Canada. Hunting from shelters that provide concealment and warmth allows hunters to withstand long hours in subfreezing temperatures.

hunt; and a couple of Flambeau's grazing decoys. Patrick had saved enough money to buy a new T/C Thunderhawk in-line for his first firearm. He shot his new rifle quite well, and Norm ensured that he practiced working the cocking handle and placing it into the safety notch. To release the safety, the bolt handle must be pulled back slightly and moved out of the notch.

I had been scouting the area for some time and had a plan that should ensure Patrick a chance for his first deer. Unfortunately, I had an appointment back home and had to leave in the midafternoon. I suggested a spot for Norm and Patrick to hide, and loaned them two grazing decoys that they could safely place in a nearby alfalfa field. They set up in a patch of brush near a trail that paralleled a barbwire fence on a steep hillside. I had seen many deer use this trail as they moved from heavily wooded coulees to the crops to forage. Norm and Patrick were wearing complete camo outfits, and they took

The author's friend, Norm Fradet, and his 12-year-old son, Patrick, pose with Patrick's first deer. The 10-point buck was decoyed into range using two Flambeau grazing doe decoys.

advantage of the vegetation to form a good blind.

Not long after they settled in, they spotted movement on the hillside. A group of deer was heading downhill toward the field. Excitement built as the whitetails slowly approached. Finally, a large doe jumped a nearby fence and stood looking at the decoys. Norm whispered for Patrick to shoot. The boy had the rifle up to his shoulder, but he didn't shoot. Norm grew perplexed. He knew the doe wouldn't stand so perfectly very long. The seconds ticked by. Still no shot! Finally, the deer moved into the brush and out of sight. Norm asked Patrick what was wrong. Patrick had been unable to get the cocking handle out of the safety notch.

He continued to pull, and just as he got the handle clear, a beautiful buck launched itself over the fence and stood in the same spot the doe had just left. Patrick still had the rifle shouldered, so he lined up the open sights and killed his first deer with a well-placed shot. When I returned home that evening, a message from Patrick was on our answering machine. I could hear the excitement in his voice as he gave me the good news.

Sharing a Secret Spot

Another interesting story involving deer decoys happened during a Mid-Morning Outfitters trip to an area we had never hunted before. The hunt started in typical style. Chopper, our fearless leader, insisted we all wear blaze-orange hunting suits instead of the camo outfits we had brought along. He thought there was a moose season taking place in this particular zone, and because rifle-toting moose hunters had to wear orange, so did we. At the end of a frustrating day, during which we had stuck out like orange blobs among large round hay bales, we met a conservation officer. He grinned and asked why we were all wearing blaze orange when we could be wearing full camo. Chopper mumbled something about the moose season, and the officer laughed. That season was long over. So much for trusting our leader to understand the hunting regulations.

The next day we switched to camo and started to see deer. Around mid-afternoon we placed deer decoys at promising locations and settled in for the hunt. The decoys worked for some of the crew, and we killed deer. That evening, we discussed how

things turned out and made plans for the next morning. We were staying in a farmhouse in excellent whitetail habitat, and we had the area to ourselves.

Early the next morning — as in pre-dawn, which is extraordinary for the Mid-Morning Outfitters crew — we prepared to head out. Chopper elected to stay in bed because he was feeling a bit ill, but he was kind enough to tell me about a great hunting spot he had found the previous evening, so off I went. Using a flashlight, I found the deer trail he suggested. It wound for a mile or so through a huge aspen bluff. Near the far end, Chopper had seen deer feeding in a hidden corner of an oat field. As dawn arose, I could see I was close to the corner of the field, so I silently skulked to the edge of the trees and started glassing.

Chopper was right! This was a great spot! No sooner did I get the binoculars focused than I spotted a nice buck and a doe about a quarter-mile away. The buck appeared to be tending the doe, which made sense because the rut was about to kick in. I sneaked back into the trees and cautiously worked toward them, using as much cover as possible. Three or four times I checked to ensure they were still in the same low part of the field. They were! The doe continued to feed and the buck stood watch to one

Decoys can be an effective tool for drawing deer into range. However, the author found out that decoys can sometimes fool the hunter as well as the hunted.

side. Sometimes I could only see their upper bodies because of a slight rise between us.

Finally, when I had gotten as near as I could get, I silently planned my shot. I visualized where I would place the cross-hairs and how I would reload as quickly as possible. Because I had two tags, my plan was to shoot the buck and then try to kill the doe. Leaning my trusty in-line on a tree, I found the deer in the scope.

Strange. It looked like they hadn't moved since the last time I checked them. Then it hit me! I was stalking a pair of my own decoys.

Chopper still claims he didn't set me up, and that he had been too ill to remember leaving the decoys out overnight.

I know better. He got me good.

CHAPTER 12

Muzzleloading in Extreme Weather

Extreme cold-weather hunting is a challenge for any firearm, not just in-lines. Because most in-lines use simple mechanisms, extreme cold won't affect performance if you have prepared your rifle properly.

Sitting silently in the wet weeds, I watched beads of water move along the smooth steel surface of the rifle on my lap. Each droplet got larger as it ran down the barrel, finally reaching the muzzle of my MK-85 and then falling away. Blasts of wind drove sheets of rain into my cozy nest, but the layers of wool and wonder-fabrics kept me warm. I wiggled my toes and fingers, checking the extremities that usually chill first.

"Ten more minutes and I'm outa here," I told myself. The driving rain kept blurring my glasses. I had long since given up using the big Zeiss binoculars now slung inside my rainjacket. Unlike me, the whitetails must have had the good sense to stay home until the storm passed. Nothing was moving. With a groan, I rose to my feet, folded up the Underwood shooting sticks, hung the slopping-wet packsack on my shoulders, and started the long, muddy walk back to the truck.

After 3½ hours of heavy rain, my rifle was pretty well soaked, as was my fleece packsack and everything inside it. I had wrapped a plastic bag over the scope, but the action was wet. Water ran out of the barrel channel when I tipped the rifle downward. Although I had taped the muzzle so no moisture could get inside the bore, I still wondered if the rifle would fire. This would be a good test.

When I reached my truck, I put the safeties off, aimed the rifle into the ditch and touched it off. With a satisfying "whuump," the old Knight rifle sent mud and water flying. Discharging the muzzleloader made sense because I would have to thoroughly clean it when I got home. I wanted to know if the in-line would have fired, just in case some wayward buck had shown up. Pleased with my wet rifle's reliability, I grinned as I put it away and

Given reasonable care, in-line rifles will operate under almost any weather condition. Protecting the rifle's action with a cover, such as this one from Thompson/Center Arms, will seal out debris and moisture while still allowing the in-line to fire.

prepared to drive home. As I drove along, I directed warm air from the heater toward all the wet gear in hopes of starting the drying process.

In-line muzzleloaders are reliable hunting rifles. Given reasonable care, they operate in almost any weather conditions. As proof of this, Tony Knight once threw a loaded MK-85 into a pond, pulled it out with an attached rope, poured the water out of the barrel, switched the safeties off and fired a shot. This amazing sequence was shown in the original Modern Muzzleloading instructional tape.

Although hunters don't commonly drop a rifle into a pond or river while deer hunting, they frequently get caught in heavy rain or snow. Let's review some neat tricks to ensure your in-line rifle works no matter what the weather extremes.

Sprinkles, Rain and Downpours

If you know there's a chance of rain as you

prepare to hunt, it makes sense to bring a waterproof case to your stand. In fact, if I'm sitting in a ground blind or tree stand and can easily stash a soft gun case, I always take one along. My son thinks I'm being overprotective, but I coddle my rifles as much as possible. Of course, this won't work on days when I'm walking a lot and rain rolls in unexpectedly. When walking or sitting in rain, I always tuck my in-line's receiver under an arm so my raingear or jacket protects it. This ensures the scope's eyepiece stays dry. Always angle the rifle downward so water runs off.

Even though I try to shield the rifle, I realize a good hunting rifle should operate in any condition. Still, it can't hurt to be a bit overprotective. Covering the action and taping the muzzle will seal the in-line from snow, debris and moisture. Some excellent protective covers for in-lines help in that regard. Thompson/Center and Knight Rifles sell vinyl covers that use Velcro to keep them in place over the entire action. The in-line rifle can still be fired with these covers in place.

In addition, I usually carry one or two plastic garbage bags in my packsack. More than once I've placed my in-line inside the plastic bag to protect it

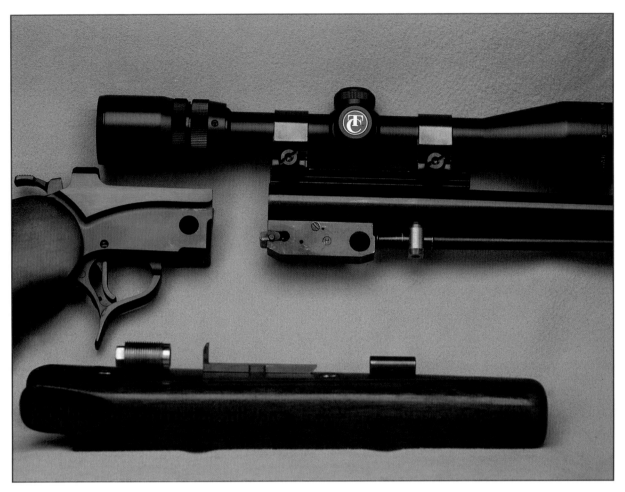

from pouring rain as I sat in a tree stand or ground blind. Another option is to drape an unopened plastic bag over the scope and receiver to ward off rain. I prefer the black or dark green bags instead of the white or orange bags, for obvious reasons.

Garbage bags and duct tape are essentials on any hunting trip. More than once I've used garbage bags as emergency rain ponchos by cutting holes for my head and arms. They also make good sitting pads on wet ground. And after a kill, we usually put the heart, liver and kidneys into a bag to keep them clean and protected until we get home.

Scope and Stock Protection

Most riflescopes should be protected during rain and snow, and lens protectors are available for nearly every scope on the market. One of the most popular are flip-up covers from Butler Creek. That company also makes a stretchy rubber pull-over cover called the Bikini. My favorite scope cover is the ScopeCoat by Devtron. This neoprene rain-jacket offers complete protection from moisture, bumps and scratches.

For the ultimate wet-weather solution for hunting optics, I use the Bausch and Lomb (Bushnell) Elite

Water-soaked muzzleloaders should be disassembled and thoroughly dried. Use a hair dryer on difficult spots, such as trigger assemblies. A light coating of oil or rust preventative should be applied to metal parts before reassembly.

4200 series of riflescopes, which have an incredible coating called RainGuard. This coating offers exceptional protection against external fogging or blurred vision caused by water-drops. Bushnell also offers the RainGuard coating to its more moderately priced Elite 3200 line. Bushnell's Elite scopes are rugged and available in several models ideal for in-line hunters. I know of several outfitters who have switched to Rainguard scopes, because they use their rifles in nasty weather. I use the 2.5-10X model, and rain and fogging are no longer a concern. I've also hunted with a 1.5-6X Elite and found it to be a great muzzleloading scope.

When muzzleloaders get drenched, they should be disassembled and thoroughly dried. Difficult spots, such as trigger assemblies, can be dried with a hair dryer, if necessary. Thoroughly clean the barrel and all other surfaces. This goes for wood

Myriad oils, solvents and protectants are available to keep your in-line operating smoothly as long as you own it. For hunting in extremely cold weather, the author suggests degreasing moving parts with a solvent or alcohol, and applying a light coating of all-weather oil to moving parts. In addition, use rust-preventative solutions on all metal surfaces.

stocks, too. Apply a light coating of floor wax inside the barrel channel to prevent moisture from soaking into the wood. If barrel channels swell and press against the barrel, significant accuracy problems result. Finally, I give all metal parts a light spray with Shooters Choice Rust Prevent before reassembling.

Sub-Zero Hunting with In-Lines

Hunting in snow and severe cold is another challenge for the hunter and the in-line. The No. 1 rule, even though it's been repeated thousands of times, is this: Never take a chilled rifle inside at the end of a hunting day. While that is good advice for any firearm, it's especially critical with muzzleloaders. Leave the rifle inside your vehicle's trunk or some other secure location that is close to outside temperature. Whenever possible, leave the rifle outside so it does not experience the extreme temperature changes that cause condensation. If you must bring your in-line inside, first wrap it inside a blanket or enclose it in a padded gun case so it warms up slowly. Remember, condensation you see on the outer surfaces is also occurring inside, so you must dry the action, barrel, trigger mechanism and all threaded parts such as nipples and breech plugs. Don't forget to check the scope lenses if you bring the rifle inside, because they will fog, hopefully only on the outside. They might need cleaning.

Extreme cold-weather hunting is a challenge for any firearm, not just in-lines. Because most in-lines use simple mechanisms, extreme cold won't affect performance if you have prepared properly. Proper lubrication is essential. Triggers will function and hammers or bolts will strike with sufficient impact to fire a cap or primer only if you've used the proper lubricant. Before hunting in extreme cold of December and January in Northern climates, degrease every moving part with solvent or alcohol. Then apply a light coating of all-weather lubricant such as Shooter's Choice CR-10. This must be placed on all moving parts, including the race-ways and trigger mechanism. Protect outside surfaces with a rust-prevention spray or silicon wipe. When these preparations are made, the rifle should be good to go.

As with rainy-weather hunting, consider "sealing" the muzzle for winter hunting, which is a good idea before any hunt. Taping the muzzle prevents twigs, snow, mud and debris from plugging the barrel. The tape has no effect on accuracy. Air trapped in the barrel between the muzzle and bullet blows the tape away long before the bullet leaves the muzzle. I've often tested taped muzzles with many types of rifles and the shot is always accurate.

Although commercial "muzzle safes" are available, I prefer a strip of electrician's tape or duct tape. Simply center a short piece on the muzzle and make evenly spaced cuts so the tape wraps cleanly along the barrel. I then wrap another strip at a right-angle over the original tape to hold it in place. In addition, wrap another length of tape, perhaps 6 inches long, around the barrel so you have replacement tape if you fire a shot. Most tape loses its ability to stick in extreme cold, so re-covering a muzzle can be difficult in extremely cold weather.

Unload or Stay Fully Charged?

One of the most important decisions muzzleloader hunters must make daily is what to do at dark if you haven't fired your in-line all day. You have only two options: empty the rifle and start fresh or leave it charged overnight. Some hunters always shoot the load into the ground, and then clean the barrel and action so they can start with a fresh charge the next morning. Most in-line hunters, however, leave the powder and bullet in the rifle and hunt with the original charge the next day. This is usually OK, and most hunters I know trust the load will be reliable and accurate.

I know of some extremes that reinforce this. One hunter told me that he left his charged, uncapped in-line inside its case and stored behind his truck seat for three months. When he got a shot during the season, the rifle killed a deer. What more can

After the hunt, muzzleloading deer hunters have two options with an unfired muzzleloader: Empty the rifle or leave it charged. In dry conditions, leaving the in-line charged, but uncapped, is sufficient. In wet weather, however, it's best to discharge and thoroughly clean your in-line rifle so there's no doubt about its readiness the next day.

you ask? However, I don't suggest leaving any rifle inside a vehicle for that length of time, let alone a muzzleloader, but this case proved his particular in-line would fire — and shoot accurately — after sitting loaded for a long time.

If the rifle has been shot, whether at a deer or to clear the barrel, cleaning is mandatory. You must clean it, period. Pyrodex and black-powder residue turns nasty when combined with moisture, so be sure to remove or displace the caustic mixture.

As a cold-weather precaution, consider switching to the hottest ignition source your rifle can use. Most manufacturers offer musket-cap nipples for their rifles. Musket caps, above left, produce more fire than No. 11 percussion caps, right.

Moisture-displacing oils prevent rust from forming, so the sooner you can clean the bore and action, the better.

Any time a fouled muzzleloader must be left uncleaned overnight, the risk of rust is high; and the longer the rifle sits uncleaned, the more likely it will rust. Serious rusting causes pitting. Pitting can be likened to pock marks, shallow areas where the steel is eaten away. If pitting occurs inside the barrel, accuracy suffers and the barrel becomes very difficult to clean. Surface pitting makes for a rough, unsightly texture that says one thing: neglect.

Also take special care to remove residue from scope mounts and rings, particularly above the nipple. Some in-line designs such as the T/C Encore have enclosed breeches so scopes and mounts don't get coated with residue, and maintenance is much easier.

Cold-Weather Ignition

Although ignition is usually not greatly affected by sub-zero weather, I've found that it will cause slightly slower velocities. My tests have shown that the variation is not enough, however, to warrant rezeroing. Some cold-weather hunters report more hang-fires, a slow ignition usually characterized by a "click-whuump-BOOM" instead of a sharp, instant explosion when flame hits the propellant.

I believe most hang-fires relate to moisture, either from condensation or a lubricant, such as oil, fouling the propellant. This can occur in the rifle's powder chamber or even inside the powder flask or container. Remember, be conservative when oiling the barrel. All that's needed is a light coating. Many rifles are stored muzzle-up, and oil inside the barrel will seep downward to the powder charge.

As a cold-weather precaution, consider switching to the hottest ignition source your rifle can use. Manufacturers offer musket-cap nipples for almost all models, and these big caps put out more fire. If you stay with No. 11 percussion caps, use the CCI Magnums because they're definitely hotter than standard caps.

No doubt the best way to ensure reliable ignition

Some cold-weather hunters report more hang-fires, a slow ignition usually characterized by a "click-whump-BOOM" instead of a sharp, instant explosion. The author, however, believes most hang-fires can be traced to moisture, either from condensation or oil fouling the propellant. Seldom is a hang-fire tied to temperature alone.

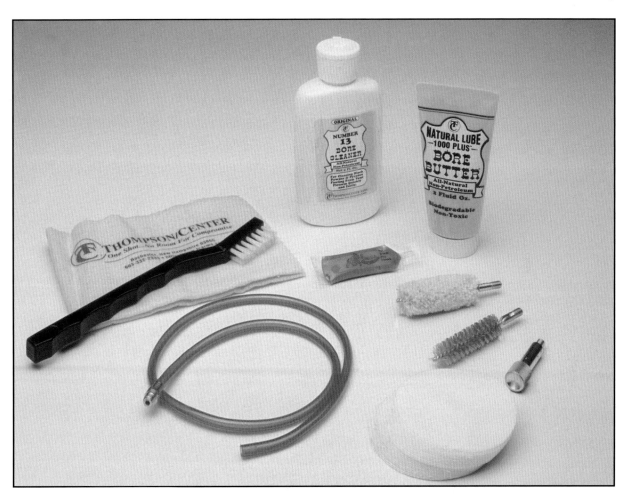

Cleaning your in-line at day's end should be routine. The job is made easier when several hunters gather to share tools, patches, solvents, oil and other equipment.

and accurate shooting is to discharge your in-line at the end of the day, thoroughly clean it, and then pop some caps or primers the next morning before loading fresh powder and a new sabot and bullet. If you're on a once-in-a-lifetime hunt, it's worth all the precautions.

Make Cleaning Part of the Routine

I'm proud to say that members of the Mid-Morning Outfitters have never had any safety or maintenance-related problems, and we hunt in all types of weather near our homes in Saskatchewan. At the end of the day, we pitch in and clean the in-lines that have been fired. Sitting in a circle, we pass around patches, solvents, oil, grease, Allen wrenches and breech-plug tools. Several hunters working together make short work of cleaning an in-line.

This work-bee is also a great time to share hunting tales and we bare souls about missed shots and spooked opportunities. We also share some amazing hunting lore during these sessions, such as how to

tell mouse scratching from the approach of a 10-pointer, and how to nap safely in your ground blind.

Most importantly, it's a great way to keep everyone focused on the hunt and the precautions necessary to be ready for any shooting contingency. The value of staying prepared is priceless.

Brian Hoffart, owner of Baitmasters Hunting Camp in northern Saskatchewan, has guided many successful in-line deer hunters during late November and early December. Temperatures and wind-chill factors can be just plain ugly at that time of year, but Brian cannot recall any of his hunters having ignition problems.

How is that possible? He has a simple rule: Every rifle is left charged but uncapped, either on the outer porch or inside a vehicle's trunk. Brian's hunters have killed huge bucks with their in-lines, which are ideal rifles for the short-range hunts Brian sets up in the big timber. When those big bucks come crashing in to rattling antlers, most hunters only get time for one shot. In-lines do the job admirably, and Brian has the pictures to prove it.

CHAPTER 13

The Traveling In-Line Deer Hunter

Muzzleloading deer hunters who travel encounter unique challenges that don't concern other hunters. Even though in-line rifles have achieved a popularity that traditional sidehammers never approached, they still require extra planning before leaving your home for that deer hunt of a lifetime.

Deer hunters have long been known to hunt whitetails far from home. This early 1900s photo shows a deer hunter on his way to the bush in northern Saskatchewan.

Autumn is deer season, the time when long-awaited dreams finally unfold. Airport terminals suddenly look like hunting lodges. Realtree and Mossy Oak outfits become common, and hard gun cases and camo duffel bags overflow from baggage carts as hunters travel to and from the field. Whether traveling to the next state or halfway across North America, deer hunters enjoy increased opportunities by taking advantage of the continent's myriad muzzleloading seasons.

In-line rifles have achieved popularity with traveling hunters that the traditional sidehammers never approached. The in-line revolution hit so strongly that whitetail outfitters no longer raise their eyebrows when told that the hunter is shooting a muzzleloader. In-lines have proven themselves from the Arctic to the Mexican desert, and special muzzleloading seasons are providing some of the best deer hunting available.

Special Challenges Await

Muzzleloading deer hunters who travel encounter unique challenges that don't concern other hunters. First, they must ensure caps and powder are available at their destination. Second, they must ensure suitable oil, patches, grease, gun-cleaning solvents and other paraphernalia are on hand. Lastly, they should ensure their guides understand the limitation of the firearm, and plan hunts

Federal regulations ban black powder and black-powder substitutes from transport on passenger airlines. The same is true of ignition caps and primers, and nonwater-based cleaning solvents. Ship these items before the hunt, or be sure they're readily available at your destination.

appropriately.

The first item is simple. Federal regulations tightly control what can be taken aboard airlines, either in carry-on luggage or inside baggage. Black powder, Pyrodex, or any substitute or similar propellant, percussion caps, musket caps and primers are strictly banned. Very simply, do not take black powder or black-powder substitutes on a flight. Do not take percussion caps or any kind of ignition device on a flight.

The same strict laws apply to solvents. They are forbidden on airlines unless they're water-based. Aerosol containers are also strictly forbidden. Gun-oil and grease are permitted, but they must be in sturdy, properly sealed containers.

Always discuss these restrictions and your requirements with your outfitter or guide, and determine how you will obtain propellants and primers. If the outfitter assures you he will have the caps and powder, don't relax until he says he has

them in hand. If he doesn't have what you need, find out how you can buy what you need before you leave the airport. This could be a shop in the city you fly into, or a gun shop en route or near where you'll be hunting. Do not take anything for granted! Your hunt can be ruined if you don't have the correct type, or adequate amounts, of powder and caps available.

Some hunts I've taken required a trip to a sporting goods store for licenses before we got started. This is a convenient opportunity to buy powder, caps and cleaning necessities — if they're in stock. Have the outfitter make sure your every need is waiting for you. Don't rely on any assurances that "Old Joe always has lots of Pyrodex on hand." Driving 50 extra miles to buy one tin of No. 11 percussion caps is a poor way to start a hunt.

The same goes for cleaning materials. Most outfitters have basic firearms cleaning gear in camp, but not necessarily the proper solvents required for black powder. Boiling water can be used as a fallback if black-powder solvent is unavailable. Your hunt will be much easier with the solvents, oil and grease you're accustomed to using. Check this out ahead of time.

Ken French, general manager of Thompson/Center Arms, has been hunting with black

powder for years. He suggests shipping propellant, caps and cleaning necessities well ahead of time so they're waiting at the outfitter's when you arrive. Shipping is inexpensive, and guarantees peace of mind.

Traveling by Air

Let's examine traveling with firearms, particularly in-line muzzleloaders. Hunters usually rely on two types of travel, in the air and on the ground. Travel involves getting to the region and then the hunt itself. Air travel ranges from major airlines, to smaller charter companies, to privately owned aircraft.

Ground travel includes everything from commercial buses, to privately owned or rented automobiles, to ATVs, to horses and mules. During all of this travel, your in-line rifle must be secure and protected from abuse.

First, find out which rules apply regarding commercial air travel with your in-line. Most airlines require that a card verifying the firearm is not loaded be signed; and some insist the card be attached to the outside of the case, while others want it placed inside. Be prepared to open your gun case when checking in. Always ensure the case is securely locked after it's inspected by the ticket

Binoculars, cameras, laser rangefinders and GPS units should be transported in a carry-on bag to ensure safe and timely arrival. In addition, detachable scope mounts allow scopes to be removed for safe transport.

agent. Also ensure the card is properly filled out and signed, if necessary. Inform the employee you do not have any ammunition, powder or caps with you. I'm always amused when going through the ritual of opening the gun case and showing the firearm to a young ticket agent whose only knowledge is that "it's long and shiny so it must be some kind of gun." After the inspection, some airlines place a "Firearms" sticker on each gun case, perhaps to ensure the baggage-gorillas give the case "special" handling.

Commercial air travel has a reputation for destructive baggage handling, and I've heard countless horror-stories of broken rifle stocks and barrels protruding through the sides of plastic cases. I have two game plans for traveling with firearms: try to make them baggage-handler proof or disguise them so the container doesn't shout "Guns!" Although you might like their look, don't plaster decals or stickers from gun manufacturers, hunting outfitters or any gun-industry related business onto your gun case. Low key is the best way to travel with fire-

Ground travel includes everything from commercial buses, to privately owned or rented automobiles, to ATVs, horses and mules. During all of this travel, your in-line rifle must be secure and protected from abuse.

arms. The bottom line is that you want your in-line rifle to reach the destination when you do, and to get there in good condition.

After your rifle and gun case pass the airline's inspection, I recommend you wrap a strip of duct-tape around each latch and snap for extra assurance. I carry a roll of tape in a carry-on bag for that job. I've seen gun cases with broken latches and torn hinges coming down baggage carousels. If a handle or latch opens, the automated-handling machinery will frequently shear it off. If possible, padlock everything shut, including your duffel bags and suitcases. I always carry a Cabela's fleece pack-sack as a carry-on, plus my camera bag. I put my binoculars, laser rangefinder and GPS into the pack-sack, along with some reading material. This ensures my optics and photo gear arrive with me, and in proper working condition.

Most hunters pack their gear into duffel bags. I've found that the Filson line of bags, although more expensive, are the best on the market. I once had a lower-quality brand bag split open on a conveyor belt in Newark, N.J., so I know what it feels like to wonder if your gear is intact. My Filsons have been through hell and back, and they still look like new.

Also make sure you have rugged name-tags for your luggage to supplement the cardboard airline tags. Don't rely on those tie-on or tape-on versions supplied at the ticket counter.

After Your Commercial Flight Arrives

Once your commercial flight arrives, your next challenge begins. Although smaller private planes might have room for hard cases, most pilots of small aircraft prefer you use a more compact soft case for luggage and gun cases. Whenever possible, hang around to ensure the firearms are handled last, so they'll be placed atop the cargo load. Always discuss the need for soft gun cases with your outfitter.

Ground travel might require both soft and hard-style gun cases. One popular case that works for both needs is the Kolpin gun-boot. After you've arrived in camp, you'll probably require a case for toting your in-line to the hunting area. Check beforehand to see what the guide recommends. Some jurisdictions require all firearms to be cased when transported on ATVs. Similar rules often apply for any motorized vehicle, or for travel through restricted areas such as parks or game preserves. I always take a silicon-treated gun sock or a water-proof soft case for traveling to and from the field. Many outfitters have spare gun socks or cases for their clients to use, but don't count on it. There might not be enough to go around, and if you get caught transporting a gun illegally, you'll pay, not the outfitter!

Choosing a Gun Case

Obtain the best quality hard gun case you can afford. It makes no sense to rely on a $29 plastic special to protect your valuable rifle from extreme conditions. I'm always amazed when I see a hunter place a rifle and scope combination that costs more than $1,000 into a cheap plastic case. Companies like Browning, Pelican, Cabela's, Americase and Starlight build cases that stand up to abuse and offer total protection to your firearm. Make sure the case also has adequate locks and good seals to keep out dust and moisture.

Most gun cases are rectangular plastic or metal boxes with a hinged lid and a shock-absorbing foam interior. One case, the Tuffpac by Nalpac Industries, is radically different from the rest. I think the Tuffpac is in a class by itself as the best case for a traveling hunter. First, the Tuffpac disguises its contents by appearing nothing like a standard gun case. They resemble containers that hold a set of golf clubs. The Tuffpac is simply a tube with a securely locking lid. They have carrying handles at the horizontal balance point, as well as a drag handle for wheeling them about.

The basic Tuffpac principle is to use soft padding inside the tube to protect your firearm. What kind of soft padding? I pack mine with a down vest, shirts,

Most hard gun gases are rectangular in shape, made of plastic or metal, and feature a hinged lid and shock-absorbing foam interior. When choosing a case, the author looks for impervious seals that prevent water and dust from reaching the rifle. This is a vital feature if the case is exposed to the elements during transport, such as in an outfitter's truck bed or roof-top carrier.

parka, socks and whatever else I decide to put in. Then I insert my firearm, which just happens to be inside a soft padded gun case. Add more padding, your boots and other gear, and lock it up. As you can see, the Tuffpac eliminates at least one piece of baggage, which is a bonus for travelers. When other hunters see the Tuffpac, they usually ask if I'm hunting with a bazooka or shoulder-fired missile, but then they ask where to buy a similar case.

Another useful gun case for traveling with in-lines is the Flambeau take-down case. These cases are designed to carry double-barreled shotguns that have been disassembled. They're perfect for an in-line rifle that has been taken apart. Take-down cases are just over one-half the length of regular cases, so they're much easier to handle.

Let's look at an important design feature that is

Continued on Page 178

Check List: Essentials for In-Line Rifles

__ powder flask	__ powder measure	__ capper
__ nipple pick	__ patch puller	__ bullet puller
__ short starter	__ No. 11 caps/musket caps	__ jag
__ take-down tool	__ Allen wrenches	__ speed-loaders
__ bullets/sabots	__ breech-plug lube	__ patches
__ solvent	__ gun oil	__ powder/pellets
__ No. 209 shotshell primers	__ DISC adapter discs (if relevant)	

Check List: Non-Essentials for In-Lines

__ range rod	__ Chapman screw driver set	__ multi-tool
__ cleaning rags	__ small hammer	__ old tooth brush
__ small folding knife	__ wooden palm saver	__ decapper
__ paper clips	__ pen/paper	__ targets
__ spare breech plug and nipple	__ spare scope	

Check List: Comprehensive Hunting Trip Checklist

__ personal gear	__ rifle and scope	__ tags, licenses
__ correspondence	__ airline tickets	__ room reservations
__ vehicle reservations	__ ammo (60 rounds)	__ spare rifle/scope
__ cleaning kit	__ gunsmithing tools	__ hard gun case
__ soft gun case	__ binoculars	__ spotting scope
__ laser rangefinder	__ GPS unit	__ compass
__ knife	__ multi-tool	__ flashlight
__ new extra batteries	__ fluorescent tape	__ game bags

__ first-aid kit: tweezers, disinfectant cream, pins, aspirin, chapstick, band-aids, dressings, insect bite relief, athlete's foot spray, laxative, cold-relief medication, large bandages, moleskin for blisters, emergency blanket

__ hunter education certificate	__ lighter	__ pack frame (optional)
__ fanny pack	__ water bottle(s)	__ extra rope
__ small meat saw	__ candy bars	

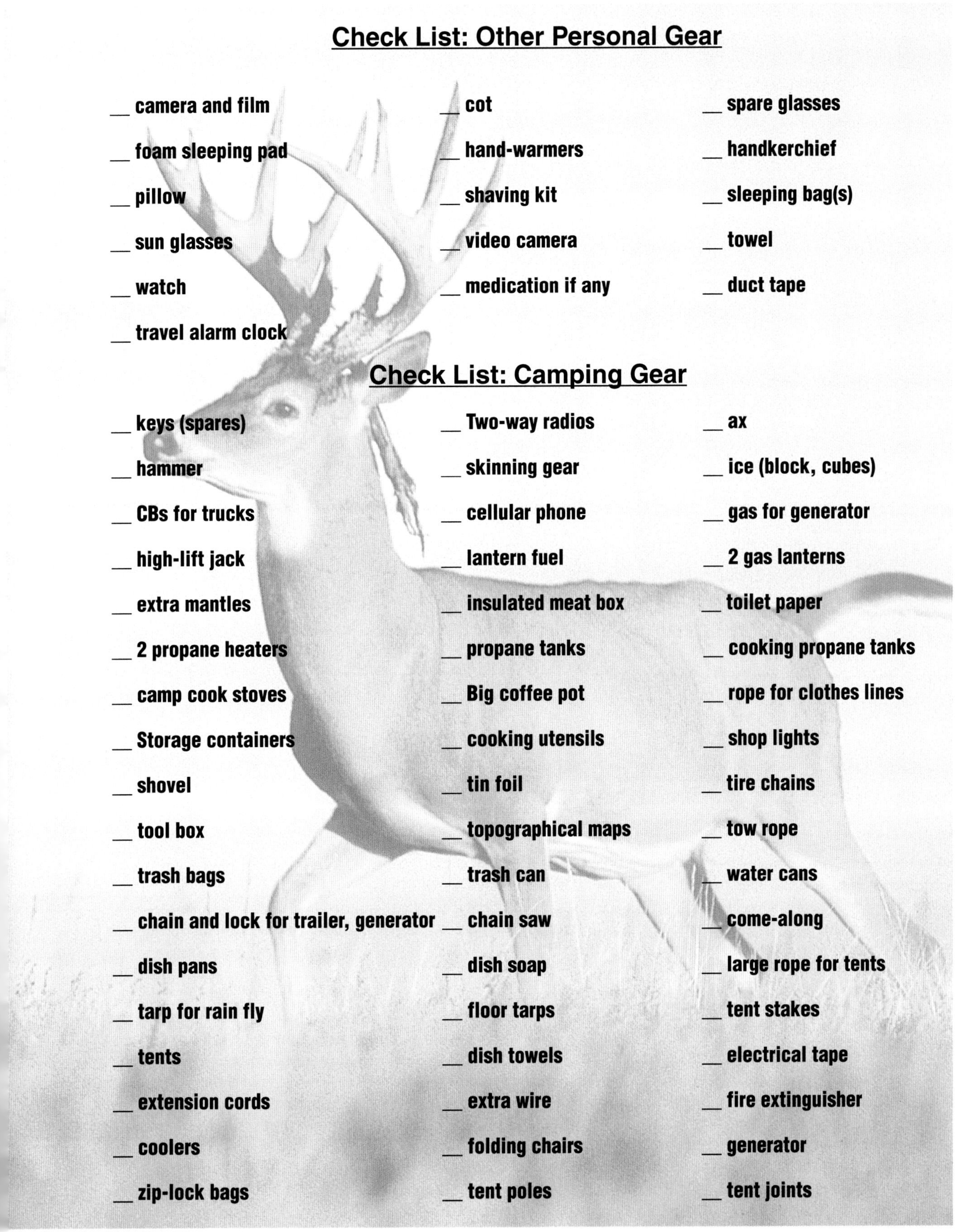

Check List: Other Personal Gear

__ camera and film

__ foam sleeping pad

__ pillow

__ sun glasses

__ watch

__ travel alarm clock

__ cot

__ hand-warmers

__ shaving kit

__ video camera

__ medication if any

__ spare glasses

__ handkerchief

__ sleeping bag(s)

__ towel

__ duct tape

Check List: Camping Gear

__ keys (spares)

__ hammer

__ CBs for trucks

__ high-lift jack

__ extra mantles

__ 2 propane heaters

__ camp cook stoves

__ Storage containers

__ shovel

__ tool box

__ trash bags

__ chain and lock for trailer, generator

__ dish pans

__ tarp for rain fly

__ tents

__ extension cords

__ coolers

__ zip-lock bags

__ Two-way radios

__ skinning gear

__ cellular phone

__ lantern fuel

__ insulated meat box

__ propane tanks

__ Big coffee pot

__ cooking utensils

__ tin foil

__ topographical maps

__ trash can

__ chain saw

__ dish soap

__ floor tarps

__ dish towels

__ extra wire

__ folding chairs

__ tent poles

__ ax

__ ice (block, cubes)

__ gas for generator

__ 2 gas lanterns

__ toilet paper

__ cooking propane tanks

__ rope for clothes lines

__ shop lights

__ tire chains

__ tow rope

__ water cans

__ come-along

__ large rope for tents

__ tent stakes

__ electrical tape

__ fire extinguisher

__ generator

__ tent joints

Most outfitters provide a time and place to check accuracy and zero your scope before the hunt. This also allows the outfitter to assess your marksmanship.

rarely considered when comparing gun cases: water and dust seals. After one hunt, the hunters I was with had to strap several hard gun cases onto a van's roof. During the journey, we hit heavy rain for several hours. All of the gun cases on the roof leaked except one well-sealed model. Most of the rifles got thoroughly soaked, and they would have rusted if we had not checked them that evening. I admit that driving 60 mph in heavy rain is a severe test, but it's the kind of abuse that occurs on hunts. I like to see heavy rubber seals around the case's shell, as is found in the excellent Pelican and Browning cases.

Getting Your Gear Home

Before concluding our discussion of travel tips, let's discuss getting home. Although traveling to the hunting area is the first priority, returning home is often too easily overlooked. You must plan ahead for how you will handle the additional baggage of antlers and frozen meat. Find out how much assistance the outfitter will provide in packaging the

rack and cape, and freezing the meat. One great idea is to travel with a large, insulated cooler that carried your large duffel bag and other gear on the way out. On the return trip, simply put your meat into the cooler and your gear into the duffel(s). Always plan to return with more than you had when you arrived.

Ensuring Your Hunt is Productive

Most outfitters follow a routine with each new batch of hunters. After completing the paperwork and settling up, you must sit down with your guide and discuss your upcoming hunt. If he doesn't make the first move in this critical step, make it for him. This is the time to make sure the guide knows your expectations, requirements, experience, and how much effort you wish to put into hunting. He must also understand your personal limitations, as well as those of your firearm. If he doesn't understand these limitations, both of you might be in for a rough time. If for some reason you haven't asked before, find out now if he has guided muzzleloading deer hunters before. Ensure he is aware of the in-line's one-shot limitations, and honestly explain your capabilities with your in-line.

Also be sure to check your rifle's accuracy before the hunt starts. Every hunter requires reassurance that the scope is still zeroed. Zeroing is also an opportunity for the outfitter and guide to assess your marksmanship and firearms competence. As always, after the shooting session, thoroughly clean your in-line and ensure you have replenished your hunting kit with powder, caps and bullets.

Detachable scope-mounts are a great asset to traveling hunters, because they allow the scope to be removed and packed separately. This ensures your scope does not get damaged. Modern scopes are tough instruments, but why take a chance if you don't have to? I frequently remove my scopes for airline trips, and use the sighting-in opportunity to reconfirm the scope and rifle are zeroed. Detachable mounts also enable me to take along a backup scope, just in case. In reality, we frequently bring a backup scoped in-line for each pair of hunters to guarantee we will not be without a rifle.

Of course, I don't always take along a spare, and on one of those hunts my rifle went missing. I arrived at our destination and soon learned my in-line had been misplaced and did not arrive with the rest of my luggage. My only option was to share a rifle with my partner. This worked out, but it meant using a scope that was not adjusted for my eyes, and a different model of in-line than I was used to.

Killing a trophy shouldn't be your only emphasis when hunting with an outfitter. Good hunts include a multitude of memories and experiences.

Time to Pack

The preparation for hunting trips comes down to selecting clothing and equipment that is useful and appropriate. Most hunters take too much stuff, and invariably wish they hadn't. Unfortunately, the best way to learn about this tendency is to make the mistake a few times, and then start adjusting.

There are essentials to take on every trip. List them and then work down in priority and usefulness. Besides standard hunting gear, in-line hunters must have necessary cleaning materials to ensure the rifle functions properly and does not rust. Every traveling hunter should create a checklist to ensure nothing is forgotten. Review these lists after each trip to add or remove items.

On pages 176 and 177 are check lists of in-line essentials and basics we use for a variety of hunting trips. The items listed, of course, can be modified considerably according to the length and type of hunting trip planned.

Anyone traveling to their first outfitted deer hunt should make an extra effort to enjoy the experience. Try not to focus only on killing a deer. We don't hunt only to kill. Making a kill often isn't part of the hunt. Good hunts include a multitude of memories. They can produce not only a 10-pointer for the wall, but memories of the one that got away.

CHAPTER 14

Photography Tips for Deer Hunters

Make your photos something you'll be proud to show friends and family. Photographs preserve memories of your trophies, equipment, weather, hunting buddies, hunting area and any other detail you wish to preserve. Framed prints, photo albums, slide shows and videotapes become important trophies themselves.

All of us photograph our hunts in our minds, but those images can't be easily shared with friends and family, and they don't last as long as images recorded on film. Photographs preserve memories of your trophies, equipment, weather, hunting buddies, hunting area and any other detail you wish to preserve. In fact, framed prints, photo albums, slide shows and videotapes become important trophies themselves.

But here's a basic reality concerning cameras and hunting: You cannot hunt and photograph at the same time. Period. It just doesn't work. Plan your photography sessions around down time, or after shooting your whitetail. Also, try to share photo-taking responsibilities to maximize those once-in-a-lifetime opportunities.

Choosing Cameras

What kind of cameras work best for recording your deer hunting memories? Two types of 35 mm cameras are commonly used on hunting trips. These are the "point-and-shoot" units and the single lens reflexes, or SLRs. Point-and-shoots are smaller and simple to operate, and some have zoom lenses to vary the photo's perspective. These little cameras usually do everything automatically for the hunter, such as wind the film, focus the lens, and rewind the exposed film at the end of a roll.

SLR cameras have lenses that can be changed, allowing a variety of specialized photos to be taken, including close-ups, wide-angle and tele-photo. Although today's SLR cameras are featherweights compared to their predecessors, they're still heavier,

Think about the finished product as you take photographs. Imagining what the final picture will look like will help you take better photos.

bulkier and somewhat more complicated to operate than point-and-shoots.

For most hunters, the point-and-shoots are the best choice because of their small size and excellent performance. Buy the best model you can afford, and use ASA 200 to ASA 400 film, which allows you to shoot photos in a wide variety of light and weather.

Taking Quality Photos

Because I've been photographing even longer than I've been muzzleloading, I've discovered many essential photographic tips. To ensure good results, think about the finished product as you take the photos. In your mind's eye, imagine what the developed slide or print will look like. What follows are some other considerations for hunters to remember.

Think Composition: Composing the subject is extremely important in creating quality photos. Avoid centering your subject in the frame. Artists use a technique called "the rule of thirds." Imagine the

camera's viewfinder is divided into thirds, horizontally and vertically. Always try to put the subject, or the horizon, at one of the intersections of those imaginary lines. For some reason, the human eye finds this more pleasing than subjects that are centered.

Think Format: Format means how you lay out the picture — vertically or horizontally, which means you must hold the camera flat or at 90 degrees. To determine what will look best, examine the scene you're about to shoot. Are most of the lines horizontal, such as a deer lying sideways in the snow with your partner kneeling by its head? Or are most of the lines vertical, such as a deer lying in the snow facing the camera, with your partner kneeling by its head? To make sure everything looks right, tip your camera 90 degrees when your subject is vertical. After you do this for a while, you will automatically think, "Vertical or horizontal shot?" Eventually you won't even think about it. You will instinctively shoot the most appropriate format.

Framing Your Shot: Set up the photo so a tree or similar object is in the foreground or along one side of the viewfinder's field of view. This will generate a

feeling of depth in your photo. Such "framing" is simple to do and gives a professional look to your picture.

Shoot Unusual Perspectives: Get down on your knees or even your belly for some of your shots. The most boring pictures are usually taken straight on by a standing photographer. Try unusual camera angles and layouts so that your photos don't all look the same.

Hold Steady: Camera movement ruins sharpness. Depress the shutter slowly and smoothly, like squeezing a trigger. Don't jab it. Most people hold the camera with their elbows away from the body, which creates an unsteady shooting platform. Drop your elbows so they're down and against your body to steady the camera. Even better, steady the camera by resting it on or against any available solid object.

Watch the Light: Keep the light from the sun over your shoulder. Light that comes from behind the camera provides the best colors. Also, certain times of the day are better than others for photographing.

Early-morning and late-afternoon light produces the richest colors and top-notch photography. Midday light tends to be flat light and often

When composing a photograph, imagine the viewfinder is divided into thirds horizontally and vertically. Try to place the subject or the horizon at one of the intersections of those imaginary lines. In this photo, the horizon rests on the lower third of the image, and the deer is offset to leave open the right third of the image.

produces heavy shadows on your subjects.

Avoid Raccoon Eyes: Bright sunlight makes people squint or pull down the brim of their caps. Tip hats or caps upward or remove them entirely. And remove those sunglasses! How do professionals get such nice light under the brims of hunters' caps?

It's really simple: Use a flash. Any flash will help, but don't get too close to your subject or you'll "white" them out.

One tip about using a flash unit for photos of dead deer: avoid having the deer's eyes looking directly at the flash. Turn the head so the eyes won't reflect light, which makes them look like glowing spots. Also, split a piece of Kleenex tissue and drape a thin layer over the flash to diffuse the light. This works great for close-up shots.

Framing your photograph with a tree or similar object in the foreground or along one side of the viewfinder generates a feeling of depth and gives the picture a professional appearance.

Other Considerations

If you hunt alone, you can take excellent self-portraits by using a small tripod and the timers built into most cameras, even many of the point-and-shoot models. Use your imagination and try many different angles and backgrounds when placing the camera to compose self-portraits. This might sound complicated, but it often is a much better way to obtain quality photos than entrusting the camera work to whoever happens to be available.

In many cases, however, you will have others nearby who will shoot photos for you. Proceed with caution if you don't know their photography skills. Ask the person to pose with your deer first. This allows you to focus the camera and determine the best composition and the location from which to take the picture. Then, explain your camera's operation to your guide or partner, including precise instructions about how you want the picture framed.

Photograph the deer from several angles, for yourself and, possibly, your taxidermist. A variety of good photos of the head and shoulders enables a taxidermist to do a more accurate job. He will appreciate receiving some photos for future reference.

Cameras are fairly rugged instruments, but they hate moisture and dust. Keep your camera in a protective case as much as possible, particularly when traveling. Always carry a plastic bag with your camera to protect it from rain and dust. Remember to put fresh batteries into the camera before a hunt, and carry at least one spare set.

Also consider your film, whether it's in the camera or stored inside a pack. Don't let film get hot. Before a trip by air, go to a photo shop and ask for some transparent film canisters so you and the security folks can see what type of film you're using. Keep spare film in these plastic canisters, and put exposed film back into them. Make a habit of storing and carrying film in standard locations so you won't misplace irreplaceable photos.

What about airport X-rays? Put your film in the transparent film canisters and then place them inside clear plastic bags. Show the bags to the security person and request it be hand-carried around the X-

Sunlight makes or breaks most wildlife photographs. Light that comes from behind the camera almost always provides the richest colors. In addition, certain times of the day are better than others for photographing. Early morning and late afternoon are often the best times. Sunlight at the edge of day provides a rich, gold hue.

Patrick Durkin photo

Photos taken in the field soon after the kill are far better than shots of the deer lying in the back of a vehicle or your back yard. Clean up the deer, and try to capture the look of the habitat where you were hunting.

ray machine. Don't take a chance, regardless of assurances film will not be damaged.

Photographing a Deer

Photographing your deer is important, and a few simple considerations make a huge difference in results. Your photos should show your respect for the animal. Photos taken in the field soon after the kill are far better than shots of the deer lying in the back of vehicles or your backyard. Remember, each deer provides once-in-a-lifetime photos, so make the effort to ensure they're great images.

Always clean up the animal. Wipe away blood from all visible areas on the deer, and remove leaves or snow that show blood. This is simply a matter of respect. You want those who view the photos to concentrate on the deer, not its spent blood. If necessary, move the deer to a cleaner, more scenic location. Consider light, background, and ease of positioning the carcass. Push tissue into wounds and

the nostrils to stop further bleeding. The simplest way to ensure the tongue is not hanging out and detracting from the deer is to cut it off and discard it. Whenever possible, photograph the deer before it's field dressed. Obviously, avoid showing the gut pile in the photo's background.

Place the animal in as natural a body position as possible. If possible, arrange the front legs in a tucked position under the brisket. Hold the head upright and avoid placing your hands in the foremost position on the rack, because your hands will look oversize. Sit or kneel behind the head and neck, and try to get vertical (head-on) photos and horizontal (sideways) shots.

Look down at the trophy for some shots, and try a few looking at the camera or just to one side. If you're with a guide, friend or family members, always get a shot of them with you and the deer. Don't sit on the deer, or kneel far behind the head. Because cameras and photos don't have depth perception, posing far behind the head can give the impression that the rack is much larger than it is in reality. This old photographer's trick doesn't fool anybody. If your trophy has antlers, photograph the rack from several perspectives to emphasize the size and shape of the main beam and tines. And remember to smile, even if you're exhausted or uncomfortable.

Hold your in-line rifle in a comfortable position, but don't allow the muzzle to angle toward the camera, yourself or another person. Ensure the optimum side for identifying the model and scope are toward the camera. Believe it or not, many hunters instantly look for such information in a photo. If you place the rifle on the deer, ensure the muzzle is angled to a safe position. Frequently, safe positioning of the muzzle looks unsafe in a photo if the muzzle angles toward you or another person in the least. Check this every time. First. Too many photos show a great buck, happy hunters and a rifle barrel apparently sticking up someone's nostril. Next, check the background so it shows the type of terrain you hunted, and perhaps where you shot from. If weather permits, remove camouflage or drab jackets if you have a brightly colored shirt or sweater underneath. Bright colors improve photos when the light is dull or the background is drab.

Try to prop the deer in as natural a position as possible. Use rocks or sticks to support the neck if it's too heavy to hold up. Holding a head in position is tiring, and time must be allowed for rest breaks. Again, think about the finished image, and make an effort to ensure the photos will be something you'll be proud to show your friends.

Video Cameras

Many hunters are using video cameras to capture their hunts. Video production can be a complicated challenge, but there is one important rule of thumb: Use a good tripod whenever possible. Although many video cameras are extremely small and light, they all work best from a tripod. Another good tip for budding cinematographers is to think about continuity. Try to shoot enough activities of your hunt that you can put together an interesting production that tells the story.

Shoot a variety of material, such as close-ups of people and activities, panoramic scenes, travel scenes and, of course, lots of hunting action. Limit your "shots" to about 10 to 15 seconds, unless you're following action as it unfolds. Shoot as much footage

Take time to place the deer in a natural position before photographing. Sit or kneel behind the head and neck and hold the rack near the base. When photographing the deer head on, as in the photo above, a vertical format often works best. Use a horizontal format when photographing the deer from the side.

as you have tapes, but remember that your edited movies should not be too long. Fifteen to 20 minutes is about right.

These tips will help you make better hunting pictures and videos, which will ensure your in-line deer hunts are preserved for a long time.

CHAPTER 15

Other In-Line Hunting Possibilities

Although the white-tailed deer is the No.1 big-game animal in North America, and the primary focus of in-line deer hunters, it isn't the only animal that's fun to hunt with black powder. Allow me to digress a bit and discuss some other fun hunting opportunities.

Modern Muzzleloading Photo

Jim Shockey has taken nearly every species of North American big game with his Knight in-line rifles.

In-line muzzleloading rifles are great for deer hunting and, for the most part, designed with deer hunters in mind. Even though white-tails are the most widely hunted big-game animal in North America, they aren't the only game in town. Many other critters walk this great continent, and the in-line rifle is capable of taking almost all of them. Elk, bears, moose, antelope, mule deer, predators and varmints all provide great challenges for in-line muzzleloading hunters.

I suspect black bears are the second most popular big-game animal hunted by in-line rifle shooters. Although not as widely distributed as whitetails, black bears are hunted from the Caroli-nas to the frozen North Woods. Similar techniques are used for both animals, depending on the region, from raucous trailing hounds to dead-quiet stand-hunting. The intent is always to get hunters close enough for a well-placed shot. Let's look at a typical Northern black bear hunt.

Bear Hunt, Saskatchewan Style

My son, Glen, and I have made several successful in-line muzzleloading rifle hunts for bruins. I suspect the reason our Mid-Morning Outfitters has not operated in bear country is that Chopper, our leader, is deathly afraid of the critters. Equally important, he is not interested in eating one.

A hunt Glen and I shared a few years ago turned into a misadventure that would have done the Mid-Morning Outfitters proud. Although we hunted with a real outfitter, we almost

***The author's son, Glen McMurchy, shot this black bear
with his Knight MK-85. Black bears are popular quarry
for in-line muzzleloader hunters.***

managed to turn a great opportunity into disaster. Our friends Brian and Sylvia Hoffart operate one of the best whitetail, bear, moose and waterfowl operations in western Canada. We hunted with them in early May, and the bears had just started hitting baits. Brian had done his homework, and he knew where a big bear was hanging out. When Brain says "big," the critter is a dandy. Huge tracks headed into one particular bait site, and Brian's bait-drum was tipped over every time he checked. He was hauling a lot of goodies to the spot.

On the first day of our hunt, we traveled into the forest in a trusty Pug, an all-terrain vehicle. We drove right to the bait and Brian noisily refilled the near-empty barrel. Brian likes to advertise that lunch has been served. Fresh scratch and bite marks marked the trunk of the aspen tree the barrel was chained to. The ground was torn up for several feet around the tree, and we spotted several large bear scats in the clearing. Three trails came into the site, each about equal in wear. This place was good!

Springtime in the forest is one of my favorite times. I make an annual trip, not so much to hunt as to recharge my batteries after a long winter. I primarily wanted to share this hunt with my son, and I also hoped to shoot some hunting photos. Glen wanted to take a really big bear with his Knight MK-85 muzzleloader.

Here's where we encountered a couple of problems. First, I'm afraid of heights. Second, not many trees were large enough for tree stands, because the location was near a riverbank. Ideally, both of us would have been in a tree, but still close enough to communicate by whispering or through hand signals. There weren't any suitable tree setups, so we shared a spruce tree that offered a good view of the bait. Glen was about 20 feet up in a hang-on stand, and I was below him in a 10-foot high ladder stand. Unfortunately, the gap and angle between us didn't allow us to communicate. I wanted both of us to be able to let the other know when a bear was spotted, so I came up with this idea of tying a string from Glen's wrist to my wrist. One tug meant a bear was spotted, two tugs acknowledged.

We sat quietly for two hours, listening to forest sounds and watching the three trails. From nowhere, I suddenly saw movement to my extreme right. Slowly, a huge black bear walked into view about 35 yards from our tree. Tiny ears, huge butt, and a low-slung gut that made the legs look too short; these signs told me the bear had everything to indicate it was a trophy. He stood looking at the bait. Carefully, I pulled the slack out of our signal cord and gave a good tug. Glen didn't give two tugs back, so I gave another stronger pull

Shooting gophers and ground squirrels is a great way to introduce kids to muzzleloading. The author loads a lightweight bullet and lowers the shot charge to 25 grains. Stalking is the norm, but killing a gopher isn't.

and waited for him to reply.

Suddenly the silence was shattered by his muzzle-loader, and a cloud of white smoke hovered above me. I could see the bear was down and not moving.

"Good shot," I told Glen.

"What were you pulling on that stupid string for?" he answered. "You almost made me drop my rifle! You pulled me off the bear twice! I was watching him come in for 10 minutes before you started jerking on the string! Was that the first time you saw him? Were you sleeping?"

I admitted sheepishly that I hadn't seen the bear, and then we started laughing. What a dumb plan! We carefully got down from the stands and examined the huge trophy. It was an old male and it died in its tracks. Glen's in-line had done the trick.

In-Lines for Gophers and Squirrels

Another great spring pastime, though perhaps not as exciting as black bears, is gopher shooting with in-line rifles. Chances are, anyone who lives in gopher country learned most of their firearms skills during hunts for these prolific little ground squirrels.

Getting close to a big whitetail means a 30- or 40-yard shot, but try hitting a gopher at that distance. Usually, the little rodent is partially hidden, so the target is never big.

I cannot recommend a favorite load, but patched round-balls do an excellent job. We usually reduce our powder charges significantly, down as low as 50 grains with round-balls, which makes the rifle enjoyable to shoot. I've used Hornady's HardBalls, (saboted round-balls) with great success. Don't be surprised if you must do some slow, deliberate sneaking to get close enough for a killing shot. We frequently belly-crawl toward feeding animals or quietly watch an active hole and wait for a gopher to resurface.

Unlike blasting away with a .22 rimfire, shooting gophers with black powder does not make a lot of smoke. But it's a great challenge.

Shooting gophers is a great way to teach kids to shoot and hunt. I drop the powder charge down as low as 25 grains with a light bullet or patched ball. Youngsters love the excitement of the smoke and noise, coupled with the dust and dirt flying around the gopher hole. Kills are not the norm, but we have a lot of fun, especially before the gophers become spooky after too much shooting in one place.

Everything discussed for hunting ground squirrels can be said for hunting the various species of "real" squirrels. The difference is that hunters convert squirrels into tasty meals. "Barking" squirrels is a technique bragged about by our ancestors who toted long rifles.

Kirby Fitch poses with the huge bull elk he killed with an in-line muzzleloader. The 5-by-6 bull weighed more than 1,000 pounds and scored over 300 points on the Boone and Crockett scoring system.

decided to initiate the first call, and let rip with a semi-aggressive bull call. Waiting for an eternity, but what was actually only moments, we were rewarded with the first response of the hunt.

I glanced toward Kevin and saw he was scouring the valley below. Suddenly from out of the bush a quarter-mile away, an animal broke into a small clearing. Keeping low and moving slowly, I made my way to Kevin.

"Did you hear that?" he asked excitedly. "There it is, but I can't make it out."

Raising my binoculars, I saw movement. "It's a 5-by-5 bull!" I said.

It was 7 a.m. We immediately scoured the valley, searching for any other animals. There were none. I waited and watched as the animal fed into the clearing. I let loose another call. The bull answered immediately, but continued feeding. He seemed content feeding in the meadow, so we had to go to him. Twenty minutes passed as we made our move.

Then, for the first time, I let out a more aggressive,

deeper call. The bull immediately spun and crashed into the timber, disappearing from sight. Stunned, I whispered, "I think I just blew it. I can't believe what he just did." Kevin was silent. Suddenly the bull bugled back.

"Thank Heavens," I thought. But this bugle didn't sound the same. The bull roared again.

"This is a different bull," I whispered. "Listen how deep and raspy he is."

Just then Kevin spotted a cow on a cut line. We watched as three more cows and calves walked toward us on the trail. They would stop and look in the bull's direction when it bugled, but then kept walking toward us when I called. This went on several times. Suddenly, they were cut off as a monster bull charged from the bush and herded them back into the timber. I had only seen him for a few seconds, but in my big binoculars I could see he was a dandy bull.

For the next hour we called back and forth, but he refused to advance. Fearing he was tiring of the game, I turned up the heat. I bugled as loud, long, raspy and deep as I dared, and then ran into the trees. I slammed a 6-inch thick piece of wood against several trees, making a fracas. It worked. The bull immediately answered and noisily tore up some trees. Kevin and I stalked closer in a deadly game of cat and mouse.

Finally, we were as close as we dared. Over two hours had elapsed, and our setup was perfect. I motioned to Kevin to get situated and indicated I would call.

One call was all it took. Within minutes, I saw him coming through the timber toward us. A quick look revealed a heavy 6-point antler on the left side. I looked away, having heard too many horror stories of hunters shooting at the antlers. The bull was swinging his head low from side to side. Steam belched from his nostrils and drool slobbered from his mouth. I settled my scope on his vitals, and allowed him to keep coming.

At 20 yards he stopped broadside. He was looking right at my camouflaged form, but he looked confused. Not finding another bull, he stopped to assess the situation. I aimed my Knight Wolverine, only to realize his vitals were blocked by the few small trees between us. I waited, certain my chance would come if I were patient. Then he spun, and was gone!

I couldn't believe my eyes! I cow-called. Nothing. I calf-called. Nothing. Finally I sat up on my haunches and could just see his rear entering the dark bush 80 yards away. I grabbed my bugle and screamed into it. He cut me off halfway through my call. Next he thrashed his huge rack into some trees, spun and stamped right up the same trail again. I set my scope on him and followed his approach. When he stepped just past the same small trees that obscured him earlier, I found his lungs and squeezed the trigger. He spun and then stood wobbling from side to side. Seconds later he bolted into the timber and I heard him collapse.

The .45-caliber 280-grain Swift A-frame bullet had done its job, penetrating both lungs before shattering a rib on the far side. We found the bullet and later verified it retained 86.2 percent of its original weight. I couldn't have used a more efficient bullet. About 6½ hours later, in 75-degree temperatures, we had him loaded into my truck and were on our way home. He was a 5-by-6 bull and weighed well over 1,000 pounds. His rack scored just over 300 Boone and Crockett points.

Hunting Exotics with In-Lines

Another great in-line challenge is hunting exotic animals. I'm not talking about shooting in pens. That is not hunting. I'm talking wild, free-ranging critters that

Mike Gray, general manager of Knight Rifles, stalked to within 120 yards of this record-book mule deer before killing it with a Knight DISC rifle.

rarely see a fence and, if they do, they'll likely go over or under it as they please. Many species of exotic critters have been transplanted throughout the United States and Canada, and most outfitters who offer such hunts try hard to ensure an exciting fair-chase hunt. Wild hog and Nilgai hunts are prime examples of hunts I've taken in recent years.

Texas is a prime region for these hunts. Right or wrong, almost every animal that walks the earth has been introduced to Texas.

"We've probably got more hogs than whitetails, and we carry a lot of whitetails on this ranch," said Craig Winters, wildlife manager of the 56,000-acre Nail Ranch in central Texas. "We call 'em the poor man's grizzly."

Wild hogs have ancestors dating back to Europe. Generations of breeding between Russian hogs and feral domestic swine resulted in an interesting critter

Modern Muzzleloading photo

Although indigenous to India and Pakistan, Nilgai antelope roam wild in South Texas. A good bull will sport horns 8 to 10 inches long. Their meat is considered excellent, as outdoor writer Larry L.Weishuhn can attest.

that must be seen to be appreciated. Although black is a predominant color, wild hogs come in many color schemes. Boars are significantly larger than sows, and they're tough and just plain miserable.

Wild hogs roam in family groups, usually adult sows and offspring from different litters. Big boars are more solitary, but like most males, they enjoy the company of females, and female wild hogs are "interested" year-round. Both sexes develop tusks, but the boars grow significantly longer and sharper ones. Tusk length, body weight and possibly coloration can determine a wild boar's trophy quality. Any boar over 300 pounds is big, and huge animals reach the 400- and 500-pound range. There is one simple rule for in-line muzzleloading for hogs: Hit them hard and then hit them again until they aren't moving.

Wild hogs should not be confused with another Texas critter, the javelina. Let's just say there is no confusing the two in person. Javelinas look big, but they're a fraction of the size and weight of wild hogs.

Javelinas are native animals that share the same range as their immigrant neighbors. Big javelinas might weigh 50 to 60 pounds. Although we encountered javelinas on our hunts, they were usually not as plentiful as wild hogs.

Any muzzleloading pig-hunter should use heavy, well-constructed bullets with the stoutest powder charge that shoots accurately. Big boars have a super-tough gristle "shield" that forms on the front quarters. That calls for heavy duty shooting!

Another animal you'll find in Texas is the always-challenging Nilgai.

"Nilgai should be called 'blue ghosts' instead of blue bulls of Texas," muttered Mike Gil as another huge bull gave us the slip during a recent hunt. "I've hunted them for years and I still can't believe how they pull off those vanishing acts!"

Nilgai originate in India and Pakistan, and they were brought to the United States as zoo specimens. Surplus zoo stock was bought and released on large Texas ranches in the 1940s. The creatures have spread over a large area of South Texas. Free roaming Nilgai frequently form small herds of cows and calves accompanied by a bull or two. Large bulls spend a lot of time by themselves or in bachelor groups until the rut in February. They reach body weights of 550 to 700 pounds, about the same as a large cow elk.

Cows and young Nilgai are beautiful creatures, with colors similar to elk. The same cannot be said for bulls. Nilgai bulls darken in color as they mature, becoming a black hue that looks blue-gray in some light. Unlike cows, bulls have a prominently taller front end. Their gait is similar to the loping movement of jackals or giraffes. In fact, they're frequently likened to small giraffes with no necks. Nilgai bulls don't grow spectacular horns. Anything longer than 8 inches is considered a trophy. Extraordinary bulls have horns exceeding 10 inches. Only a couple of inches separate a good bull and a huge set of horns, so there's not much to work with when judging trophy size. Nilgai make interesting shoulder mounts, although "homely" might best describe their appearance. Still, the bulls provide succulent, flavorful meat that's a treat for the successful hunter.

Many Texas ranches have suitable numbers of Nilgai to accommodate guests for one- to three-day hunts. Because neither Nilgai nor wild hogs are native species, the only licensing requirement is a Texas nonresident tag.

Texas hunts are usually conducted "safari style." That is a politically correct term for truck hunting. Guides use four-wheel-drive pickups to cruise roads and trails looking for game. Once spotted, the critter can be stalked or shot at from over the truck hood or from special benches. Many operations have comfortable hunting rigs that feature elevated bench seats mounted on the box or frame of heavy-duty trucks. The plan is to see game before it sees the truck. Most sightings result in short stalks that might not result in a shot.

The habitat dictates how close you get for a shot. Because the country is much more open than wooded, be prepared for fairly long shots. Although hogs spend part of their day in cactus and other cover, they also feed in fields. Similarly, Nilgai are found in habitat ranging from wide-open flats to heavy oak forests with limited visibility.

Outfitter Bobbie Brown helped arrange a hunt on a ranch crawling with Nilgai. Many blue bulls roamed the pastures and hills, and we tried several unsuccessful stalks before we ambushed a herd as it approached a water hole. Tony Knight shot at a bull that ran off at

Using in-line rifles to hunt pronghorn antelope on the prairies can prove fun and challenging. This Colorado antelope fell to a Hornady Great Plains lead bullet fired from a T/C Encore. Colorado does not allow the use of riflescopes, sabots or Pyrodex Pellets during its black-powder seasons.

Patrick Durkin photo

the shot, but the 220-grain Swift A-Frame did the job, and the bull died within 150 yards. Later, my long-range practice sessions helped me connect on a large bull at well over 300 yards.

Obviously, exotic animals offer great off-season hunting opportunities for unique trophies. A good fair-chase muzzleloading hunt offers great sport and lots of excitement. Although success rates are usually high, no reputable outfitter guarantees a kill.

CHAPTER 16

The In-Line's Impact: Today and the Future

Muzzleloading rifles are the safe alternative for many hunters, and they're more "politically acceptable" to nonhunters because of the increased challenge of hunting with them. For those reasons and others, most analysts expect interest in modern in-line muzzleloaders to keep increasing in the years ahead.

A few years ago, I surveyed American and Canadian wildlife agencies for *Deer & Deer Hunting* magazine to obtain information about muzzleloader hunting. The magazine also asked muzzleloading-related questions in its subscriber surveys in 1994 and 1997. The comprehensive wildlife agency survey was carried out in 1998, and I have updated that information in this book as much as possible.

The *D&DH* subscriber survey indicated that the use of in-line muzzleloading rifles almost tripled among its readers from 6.6 percent in 1994 to 18.8 percent in '97. I wouldn't be surprised if that rate of increase happened again between 1997 and the year 2000, although I don't have data to support this belief. I have recently seen numbers indicating the number of muzzleloading hunters now exceeds the number of archers in the United States.

Surveying the Continent

When I conducted the '98 *D&DH* survey, all 50 states and 10 Canadian provinces responded. The results indicate that:

✓ muzzleloader hunting was still in a growth stage.

✓ muzzleloader hunting was not seen to have significant problems.

✓ muzzleloader hunting was very well regulated.

Participation in the sport of muzzleloader hunting was increasing in 45 out of 58 jurisdictions that reported, or 77.6 percent. Thirteen out of the 58 agencies, or 22.4 percent, thought participation in the sport was stable, and no

Muzzleloading Trends

1. Describe the participation level of muzzleloader hunting in your state or province.

A. *Decreasing*   0   0%

B. *Stable*   12   21.1%   Alberta, Ariz., Fla., Ga., Ind., Manitoba, Nev., N.C., Pa., Tenn., Utah, Wyo.

C. *Increasing*   45   78.9%   Ala., Alaska, Ark., B.C., Calif., Colo., Conn., Del., Hawaii, Idaho, Ill., Iowa, Kan., Ky., La., Maine, Md., Mass., Mich., Minn., Mo., Neb., N. Brunswick, Newfoundland, N.H., N.J., N.M., N.Y., N.D., Nova Scotia, Ohio, Okla., Ontario, Ore., Quebec, R.I., Sask., S.C., S.D., Texas, Va., Vt., Wash., W.Va., Wis.

2. How significant of a role does muzzleloader hunting play in deer management strategies for your state or province?

A. Not significant   14   24.6%   Alaska, B.C., Calif., Conn., Ill., Kan., Mich., Mont., Neb., N. Brunswick, Nova Scotia, S.C., Texas, Wyo.

B. Slightly significant   35   61.4%   Ala., Alberta, Ariz., Colo., Del., Fla., Ga., Hawaii, Idaho, Ind., Iowa, La., Maine, Manitoba, Mass., Minn., Mo., Nev., Newfoundland, N.J., N.M., N.Y., N.C., N.D., Ontario, Ore., Pa., R.I., Sask., S.D., Utah, Va., Wash., W.Va., Wis.

C. Highly significant   8   14.0%   Ark., Ky., Md., N.H., Ohio, Quebec, Tenn., Vt.

agencies indicated it was decreasing.

Agencies were asked to assess the significance that black-powder hunting played in deer management. Of the 58 responses received, 14, or 24.1 percent, indicated it was not significant; 36, or 62.1 percent, said it was slightly significant; and eight, or 13.8 percent, said it was highly significant. Muzzleloader hunts are being used by some agencies to manage high deer populations.

When asked to rate their "comfort level" with muzzleloader hunting and technology, 58 states and provinces responded. Most wildlife managers, 34 or 57.6 percent, said they had no concern; 21, or 36 percent, had moderate concern; and four, or 6.8 percent, had significant concerns. The results suggest managers are most worried about muzzleloading equipment and technology, and less about the effect of black-powder hunting on deer populations.

Most wildlife agencies — 52 of 58, or 89.7 percent — try to keep tabs on hunter participation, and only 6 (or 10.3 percent) do not. Similarly, 48 agencies, or 82.8 percent, monitor hunter success rates, and 10 do not. In addition, most wildlife managers — 41, or 72 percent — keep up on technological changes, while 16, or 28 percent, do not.

Further, 19 agencies, or 32 percent, said they planned or had recently changed muzzleloading regulations; and 40, or 68 percent, did not plan any changes. Virtually all agencies that were planning changes were considering more liberal seasons or certain restrictions on optics and ignition types.

Most agencies appear to monitor technological innovations, and had already implemented "appropriate" measures to address concerns.

Defining Laws

Most muzzleloading regulations deal with muzzleloading definitions. A common regulation was requiring the rifle be loaded from the muzzle. An almost equally common requirement was the use of black powder or black-powder substitute. The third most common restrictions dealt with the type of sights allowed for deer hunting. Several states do not allow telescopic sights of any kind during black-powder seasons, and a handful allow only non-magnifying scopes. The fourth most common restriction related to minimum bore diameters, which ranged from .36 in South Carolina to .50 in Washington. A few states regulate minimum barrel length, with minimums of 16 to 21 inches stipulated. In addition, three states allow only single-barreled rifles.

Muzzleloading bullets are also regulated by several states, with some allowing only lead projectiles. Other agencies set minimum allowable weights. Four states specify that only one projectile per loading is allowed. Powder charges are also controlled in a few states. How wardens enforce a load of no less than 50, 60 or 62 grains is beyond me.

Action types are also regulated. Pennsylvania allows only flintlocks. And for a short time, basically 1998,

Muzzleloading Trends

3. Does your agency have data to indicate that modern in-line muzzleloaders have increased deer harvests to the point where your state or province is considering regulation changes?

A. No data	58	98.3%	All except Virginia
B. Data available	1	1.7%	Va.

4. How would you rate your agency's "comfort level" with the current state of muzzleloader hunting and muzzleloader technology?

A. No concern	34	58.6%	Alaska, Alberta, Ariz., Ark., B.C., Calif., Conn., Del., Fla., Ill., Ind., Ky., La., Mich., Minn., Mo., Mont., Nev., Newfoundland, N.H., N.M., N.Y., N.C., Nova Scotia, Ohio, Okla., Ontario, Sask., S.D., Tenn., Texas, Utah, W.Va., Wis.
B. Moderate concern	20	34.5%	Ala., Ga., Hawaii, Idaho, Iowa, Kan., Maine, Manitoba, Md., Mass., Neb., N. Brunswick, N.J., N.D., Ore., Pa., R.I., S.C., Va., Vt.
C. Significant concern	4	6.9%	Colo., Quebec, Wash., Wyo.

Colorado outlawed in-lines during black-powder seasons. Between those extremes, a few states require the nipple be exposed to the elements or that the ignition system be of flint and/or percussion cap.

Expanding Opportunities

Since the survey, Georgia has opened a new muzzleloading season and other agencies have increased opportunities for in-line hunters. For example, Pennsylvania will allow the use of conical bullets during its flintlock season, a departure from the longstanding insistence on patched round-balls. Perhaps the most significant development in the late 1990s was Colorado's short-lived decision to ban in-lines for black-powder seasons. When the ban took effect, many individuals foresaw the decision as the first domino to fall on the in-line rifle. They predicted other states would soon follow with similar restrictions. In truth, this proved to be a domino that was standing by itself. The Colorado situation developed when a small number of traditionalists found a way to impose their will on the majority. To the credit of Colorado's wildlife agency, the domino was put back up, and the situation corrected for the next year.

How Many Laws are Needed?

The survey indicates muzzleloader deer hunting in North America is healthy and well-regulated by the agencies entrusted with managing our resources. Additional research from *D&DH* sheds even more information on the state of black-powder hunting. An interesting fact is Michigan's status as the continent's leader in muzzleloading deer hunters. In addition, 13 states account for 80 percent of the muzzleloader hunters nationally. Further, 80 percent of muzzleloading hunters primarily pursue whitetails.

These surveys leave me with a few questions. Such as, how many muzzleloading regulations do we need? Does it really matter what muzzleloader action style, bullet weight, sighting device or amount of powder each hunter uses? I prefer to let each hunter make these decisions for himself so he can enjoy muzzleloading to its utmost. The objective is to obtain a clean kill, and I'm afraid some antiquated regulations force hunters to use sights or bullets that increase the possibility of a poor shot. For example, open sights will never be as accurate as scopes, and round-balls will never be as effective as conicals or saboted bullets when it comes down to killing an animal.

The Timing of Muzzleloader Hunts

The timing of black-powder hunting seasons varies greatly between the states and provinces. Some muzzleloading seasons are held before the rifle season and some are held after. When factoring in archery and firearms seasons, wildlife agencies must do a balancing act to design season frameworks that work for everyone. Yet another consideration is the timing of the rut. Northern states also consider winter vs. fall hunting conditions, so hunters should decide what type of weather they prefer for hunting. Muzzleloading seasons also vary greatly in length, ranging from a few days to several weeks. In addition, they range from one buck only to liberal allocation of antlerless permits. With ever-changing refinements to black-powder seasons, you must get the actual regulations straight from the relevant agency.

The Future of In-Line Hunting

What is the future of in-line hunting? The answer

Muzzleloading Trends

Is your agency ...
A. ... monitoring muzzleloader hunter participation?

Yes	51	89.5%	Ala., Alberta, Ariz., Ark., Calif., Colo., Conn., Del., Fla., Ga., Hawaii, Idaho, Ill., Iowa, Kan., Ky., La., Maine, Manitoba, Md., Mass., Mich., Minn., Mo., Neb., Nev., Newfoundland, N.H., N.J., N.M., N.Y., N.C., N.D., Nova Scotia, Ohio, Okla., Ontario, Ore., Pa., Quebec, R.I., Sask., S.C., S.D., Tenn., Utah, Va., Vt., Wash., W.Va., Wyo.
No	6	10.5%	Alaska, B.C., Ind., Mont., N. Brunswick, Texas

B. ... monitoring muzzleloader hunting success rates?

Yes	47	82.5%	Ala., Alberta, Ariz., Calif., Colo., Conn., Del., Fla., Ga., Hawaii, Idaho, Ill., Iowa, Kan., Ky., Maine, Manitoba, Md., Mass., Mich., Minn., Mo., Neb., Nev.,Newfoundland, N.H., N.J., N.M., N.Y., N.D., Nova Scotia, Ohio, Okla., Ontario, Ore., Pa., Quebec, R.I., Sask., S.C., S.D., Tenn., Utah, Va., Vt., Wash., W.Va.
No	10	17.5%	Alaska, Ark., B.C., Ind., La., Mont., N.Brunswick, N.C., Texas, Wyo.

C. ... monitoring technological changes?

Yes	40	71.4%	Ala., Alberta, Ark., Colo., Del., Fla., Hawaii, Idaho, Ill., Ind., Ky., La.., Maine, Md., Mass., Mich., Mo., Mont., Nev., Newfoundland, N.H., N.J., N.M., N.Y., N.D., Nova Scotia, Ohio, Okla., Ontario, Ore., Pa., Quebec, R.I., S.C., S.D., Utah, Vt., Wash., W.Va., Wyo.
No	16	28.6%	Alaska, Ariz., B.C., Ga., Iowa, Kan., Manitoba, Minn., Neb., N. Brunswick, N.C., Sask., Tenn., Texas, Va., Wis.

Do you anticipate any changes to current muzzleloading regulations or has your agency enacted any changes recently?

Yes	19	32.7%	Ark., Colo., Hawaii, Kan., Md., Mass., Nev., N.J., N.M., N.D., Ore., Quebec, R.I., S.D.,Tenn., Texas, Va., Wash., Wyo.
No	39	67.3%	Ala., Alaska, Alberta, Ariz., B.C., Calif., Conn., Del., Fla., Ga., Idaho, Ill., Ind., Iowa, Ky., La., Maine, Manitoba, Mich., Minn., Mo., Mont., Neb., N. Brunswick, Newfoundland, N.H., N.Y., N.C., Nova Scotia, Ohio, Okla., Ontario, Pa., Sask., S.C., Utah, Vt., W.Va., Wis.

might be tied to a bigger question: What is the future of hunting? Our society does not place the same values on hunting that were common in previous generations.

In general, the muzzleloading industry is optimistic. The major players believe muzzleloader hunting is strong and getting stronger.

Muzzleloading rifles will play a major role in providing recreation for hunters in the new millennium. Ken French, general manager of Thompson/Center, said, "Muzzleloaders are perceived as being politically correct, so they will play an increasing role as acceptable hunting tools."

French said society is too fast-paced for many people to enjoy old-style hunting. People often don't take the time to develop hobbies and learn age-old skills and techniques. Although many people will stare at a computer screen and surf the Net for hours, they don't make time for shooting and hunting. This is true despite the fact that most states hold record numbers of deer, and many herds require reduction. In some regions, more deer will be killed by automobiles and starvation than by hunting. Even so, hunting is the only logical, cost-effective method of big-game population management. In reality, hunting is the only organized means to keep deer herds in a balance with their habitat.

When asked about possible changes in the future, French said propellants had not kept up with in-line

Ken French, general manager of Thompson/Center Arms, believes muzzleloading rifles will play an increasing role as acceptable hunting tools. "The bad press dumped on firearms does not extend to muzzleloaders," he said. "The public appears to feel more comfortable with muzzleloader hunting, and landowners have few concerns."

rifles, so he expected some developments in that area. He foresees cleaner burning propellants, which should entice more participants to the sport. He also believes the No. 209 shotshell primer is the ignition source for the future, because it is waterproof and reliable. Further, he believes wildlife agencies are doing a great job of regulating the sport, and does not expect to see major regulatory changes.

Part of that is because muzzleloaders will never be a weapon of choice for violators. Black-powder rifles, although becoming more modern in appearance and technology, are simply not the most effective poaching tools available because they're neither quiet, quick to load, nor effective at extreme distances when compared to all other sporting arms.

"The bad press dumped on firearms does not extend to muzzleloaders," French said. "The public appears to feel more comfortable with muzzleloader hunting, and landowners have few concerns."

More Growth Foreseen

Tim Pancurak is T/C's customer services manager. He also sees continued growth in the muzzleloader field. Pancurak is the initial contact person for customers who call T/C, so I asked him what is the most common complaint he hears from in-line shooters. He quickly responded, "Accuracy expectations."

Pancurak said many shooters don't take time to learn how to make their in-lines attain maximum performance. Lack of practice and failure to use established procedures brings complaints that the new rifle is not

shooting as well as expected. Pancurak has heard of individuals who opened muzzleloading blister-packs and went hunting without taking any practice shots or checking the sights. There is no excuse for such lazy, irresponsible behavior. We owe more to the deer, and to ourselves. Nothing can do more harm to muzzleloading than to minimize preparations and increase the chances of wounding game.

Another man I asked to weigh in on this topic was Tony Knight, the inventor/gunsmith who started the in-line revolution. An afternoon with Tony is a learning experience. He is extremely aware of trends in in-line deer hunting, and he hunts all over North America. He has watched rapid changes occur as millions of hunters entered the sport. He thinks muzzleloader hunting will continue growing.

"Muzzleloaders are the safe alternative," he said. He agrees with French's assessment that muzzleloaders are more "politically acceptable," and that muzzleloading hunters are more welcome during hunting seasons than any other type of hunter.

"Society does not have a problem with folks muzzle-

Tony Knight believes muzzleloading will continue to grow in the future. He also foresees cleaner-burning propellants and faster-shooting in-line rifles. His latest creation, the .45 Super, can achieve 2,500 feet per second when shooting a saboted .40-caliber, 150-grain bullet.

loader hunting," Knight said.

Tony also made some controversial points we should consider. Not everyone will agree with his opinions, but they're worth thinking about. Here's a sampling of the world according to Tony Knight:

✓ "Our society is taking the fun out of hunting! If we imposed all those rules on any other sport, we wouldn't have football, baseball or basketball."

✓ "How do we make hunter-ed more fun and appealing so more kids will want to enroll?"

✓ "Camo is essential for hunting, but equally important is that it allows the wearer to make the statement that he is a hunter."

✓ "Any hunting season is a good season."

✓ "Long-range muzzleloading isn't new. Our ancestors made very long shots during the Civil War and the War of Independence."

✓ "Some people are shooters, and some people are hunters."

✓ "Muzzleloading hunters should organize their essential accessories into pockets, and always put the same objects into the same pocket."

✓ "Society is breaking down. No one is passing on traditions to the kids."

When I asked Tony what changes he foresees for muzzleloading, the first thing he mentioned was improved propellants. He believes in Hodgdon Pyrodex Pellets, and rates these pellets as the perfect propellant for in-line rifles. Even so, he says, "We'll see cleaner-burning pellets that don't cause rusting concerns, as well as other advances in the next few years."

The Future of Knight Rifles?

Tony also explained the innovations behind his .45 Super DISC, which pushed in-line performance to a new level in the year 2000.

"Why not shoot bullets faster?" he asked rhetorically. "This new rifle is going to be the best in-line available for deer hunters."

The .45 Super is a slightly modified DISC rifle that features a 26-inch fluted, semi-varmint weight barrel. Knight went with a .45 bore size to accept a new saboted .40-caliber, 150-grain Barnes HP "spitzer" bullet. This projectile will be launched at 2,600 fps. The powder charge will be five 30-grain Pyrodex Pellets, or 150 grains. These smaller pellets were introduced by Hodgdon for replica black-powder revolvers that cowboy action shooters use. The pellets are packaged in cans of 100, and are the most economical pellets to date.

Tests indicate that with a 100-yard zero, the 150-grain bullet will drop four inches at 200 yards. Other bullets for this rifle will weigh 165 grains, and both RedHot and lead bullets will be available in those two weights. Plans also include thicker sabots for using .357-caliber pistol bullets.

Knight .45 Super DISC Velocities

Load: 150 grains of Pyrodex Pellets (five 30-grain pistol-sized pellets to fit the .45-caliber bore) and CCI No. 209 shotshell primer. The slugs were Barnes X-Bullets. The barrel was swabbed between shots. Five-shot strings were fired through Oehler 43 & 35P chronographs.

Distance	150-gr. Barnes	165-gr. Barnes
Muzzle (5 feet)	2,639	2,602
100 yards	2,010	2,051
200 yards	1,530	1,652

Conclusion

Every hunter should be concerned about the future of deer hunting. Shooting and hunting are activities we've taken for granted for many generations, but times are changing. I do not intend to preach about gun control and the anti-hunting movement. Instead, I implore you to take a kid hunting, either your own or another whose parents cannot offer that experience. Share your respect for nature, your love of the outdoors and your reverence for life with at least one youngster. Provide that youngster the same chance to be fascinated and awed by wild creatures. Help them understand the difference between hunting and slaughter, as well as the difference between pride and shame.

Our society is becoming overwhelmed with hassles, external pressures and moral problems. Incredibly enough, many of today's youths -- whether from the city or the country — have never watched a sunrise nor heard the life-sounds of a marsh at dawn. After all, most farm children are bused to towns or cities and spend much of their day in the concrete jungle. Our outdoor heritage is still there for everyone, if they're only lucky enough to experience it. Kids who have never fished, camped, hiked, hunted or target-practiced

Every hunter should pass on the gift of the outdoors and share every opportunity to preserve our sport. Taking a youngster hunting, or an adult who has never been, is one of the best ways to achieve both objectives.

will never know the importance of nature and the outdoors to human beings. Could you live without the outdoors?

For that matter, don't limit the invitation to children. It's no longer rare for adults to take up hunting long after their formative years. In some cases, they simply never had enough money earlier in life to properly outfit themselves for hunting. All they need now is the mentor to get them started.

Why should you do this? Well, in most cases, someone took you out the first time, right? Chances are, it was a friend or relative who gave you the gift of becoming an outdoorsman. Every hunter should pass that gift along and share every opportunity to preserve our sport. We all must realize the fragile nature of our hunting heritage, and appreciate the fact that a small, but fixated, segment of our society will never cease trying to eliminate hunting and shooting. Everyone who owns a firearm and enjoys hunting must work to ensure that such personal matters are never legislated for them.

In-line muzzleloader hunting for deer is a great sport. I sincerely hope this book proves of value to in-line enthusiasts today, and that it might start future hunters on their journey into the excitement of in-line muzzleloader hunting.

About the Author

Ian McMurchy lives in Regina, Saskatchewan, Canada, with his wife, Darlene, and two cock-a-poo "gun dogs," Winchester and Remington. Ian and Darlene have four grown children who live in the province, two in Regina and two in Saskatoon.

McMurchy took early retirement in 1996 after a career of almost 28 years in Saskatchewan's wildlife agency. He worked primarily on big-game population management, black bear management and animal damage-control.

In recent years he has worked full-time as an outdoor writer and photographer. He is a magazine field editor, and he specializes in optics, black-powder rifles, extreme-range shooting, and hunting with centerfire rifles. His photographs appear in numerous magazines, books, newspapers, catalogs, calendars, advertisements and postcards. His photos have appeared on more than 85 magazine covers, including *Outdoor Life, Field & Stream, Petersen's Hunting, Deer & Deer Hunting* and many regional publications.

He also features his photographs when giving seminars that discuss photography and hunting.

McMurchy also does consulting work for big-game outfitters. Besides working as a consultant for the outfitting operations, McMurchy helps outfitters set up and maintain Web sites. He also provides the text and photographs for their advertising displays.

McMurchy finds that retirement is not a time for rest. He has shot virtually every inline rifle, muzzleloading bullet and propellant that was manufactured through the year 2000. He works closely with major muzzleloading companies assisting with product development and field testing. This extensive field work allows him to evaluate most of today's in-lines on the range and while deer hunting.

McMurchy's writings are based on a blend of technical and field shooting. His main partner in this work is his son, Glen.

"I have been blessed with the chance to hunt a lot with my son," McMurchy said. "He gets to shoot more than I do because I'm usually behind a Nikon. At least that's my excuse. Glen has taken some monster caribou, a good mountain goat and a Saskatchewan whitetail that grossed in the high 170s. Sharing Glen's enjoyment of hunting is why I'm out there."